# STONES
# STILL
# SPEAK

# STONES STILL SPEAK

## HOW BIBLICAL ARCHAEOLOGY ILLUMINATES THE STORIES YOU THOUGHT YOU KNEW

## AMANDA HOPE HALEY

Revell

a division of Baker Publishing Group
Grand Rapids, Michigan

© 2025 by Amanda Hope Haley

Published by Revell
a division of Baker Publishing Group
Grand Rapids, Michigan
RevellBooks.com

Printed in the United States of America

Library of Congress Cataloging-in-Publication Data
Names: Haley, Amanda Hope, author.
Title: Stones still speak : how biblical archaeology illuminates the stories you
    thought you knew / Amanda Hope Haley.
Description: Grand Rapids, Michigan : Revell, a division of Baker Publishing
    Group, [2025] | Includes bibliographical references.
Identifiers: LCCN 2025002499 | ISBN 9780800746483 (paperback) | ISBN
    9780800747473 (casebound) | ISBN 9781493451470 (ebook)
Subjects: LCSH: Bible—History of contemporary events.
Classification: LCC BS635.3 .H354 2025 | DDC 220.95/05—dc23/eng/20250416
LC record available at https://lccn.loc.gov/2025002499

Cover design by Kathleen Lynch

The author is represented by Alive Literary Agency, www.aliveliterary.com.

Baker Publishing Group publications use paper produced from sustainable forestry practices and postconsumer waste whenever possible.

25  26  27  28  29  30  31        7  6  5  4  3  2  1

For Brandy's daughters: Addison, Alyssa, Audrey, and Ava

As you grow up and hear stories of your mother from old friends like me, know that her love of God made her strong when she felt weak and her love for you and your father helped her fight.

> "Listen to Me, you who pursue righteousness,
> Who seek the LORD:
> Look to the rock from which you were cut,
> And to the quarry from which you were dug."
>
> —Isaiah 51:1 NASB

# Contents

# Introduction

## Rocks Are Neither Deaf nor Dumb

Eight miles northwest of Jerusalem, on the outskirts of modern-day Ramallah along the Central Ridge Road, sits Tel en-Nasbeh. The site has been identified as the likely location of biblical Mizpah,[1] where Israel's judges fought many battles and where the prophet and judge Samuel erected a standing stone meant to commemorate an Israelite victory over the Philistines (1 Sam. 7:12). But Samuel's monument was neither the first nor the last in this area.

At least seven centuries earlier, the forefather of all Israelites, Jacob, had a habit of erecting stones. At Bethel, he had already placed one in honor of God's theophany (Gen. 28:18), and there he would later mark his wife Rachel's burial (35:20). But in the vicinity of Mizpah, Jacob made a treaty with his uncle and father-in-law, Laban: "Jacob took a stone and set it up as a pillar. Then Jacob said to his brethren, 'Gather stones.' And they took stones and made a heap. . . . Then Laban said to Jacob, 'Here is this heap and here is this pillar, which I have placed between you and me. This heap is a witness, and this pillar is a witness, that I will not pass beyond this heap to you, and you will not pass beyond this heap and this pillar to me, for harm'" (31:45–46, 51–52). Jacob

9

and Laban may have been memorializing a sort of war—an epic struggle between in-laws for authority and inheritance—but their standing stone and heap of stones had the practical purpose of marking territories. From that day forward, neither man would enter the other's lands. These stones marked the future boundary between the Northern and Southern Kingdoms of Israel, long before Israel was a nation or Jacob himself was renamed Israel. Today, they would be near the border between modern Israel and the Disputed Territory often called the West Bank.

In the ancient world—a time when most people could neither read nor write and glow-in-the-dark traffic signs were unimaginable—rocks were both abundant and everlasting. The average Bedouin hunter or herder moving past an obviously man-made monument might stop and wonder at its purpose had he not heard its origin story from his ancestors. Such a marker was often called an *ebenezer*, a Hebrew word that means "stone of help." We get that name from the prophet Samuel who "took a stone and set it up between Mizpah and Shen, and called its name Ebenezer, saying, 'Thus far the LORD has helped us'" (1 Sam. 7:12). In this instance, the stone was placed to remind passersby of God's faithfulness and help to His people in the face of the mighty Philistine army.

"Stones of help" such as those used by the Bible's patriarchs and judges are not unique to the ancient Near East. As much as a millennium before Jacob was born, the famous giant sarsen stones that make up Stonehenge were lifted into place by at least one thousand British Neolithic farmers.[2] In Australia, Aboriginal stone arrangements placed into geometric, zoomorphic, or god-like shapes were likely used for ceremonial activities prior to the continent's colonization.[3] And on the opposite side of the globe, the Inuit people of modern-day Nunavut, Canada, were creating *inuksuk* in the Arctic Circle between 2400 and 1800 BCE.

During a walk or ride along any rocky coast or public land in Canada, you are sure to see piles of rocks arranged along the path. Today locals and tourists alike select flat stones and stack them into the humanlike shapes as works of art, but they had purposes in antiquity. The word *inuksuk* means "to act as a human," although not all creations were anthropomorphic. Most stacked or upright stones were made to guide others toward good hunting lands or rich fishing waters, or to warn them away from predators or natural dangers. Those shaped like humans, which are more accurately called *inunnguaq*, served the same purposes but also had spiritual significance.[4]

In all these cultures, stacked and standing stones were neither deaf nor dumb. They were silent witnesses to early human activities, and for millennia they have steadfastly spoken the truths of history.

As technology progressed and humans produced bronze and iron tools that could shape the earth's natural stones into functional building blocks, monumental stelae, modest kitchen vessels, and even delicate jewelry, stones became valued for what they could become rather than what they inherently were. Today, the stones of the ancient world speak to us not only as simple markers of momentous but often forgotten events, but also as bold evidence of how life was lived.

Stones were the literal and figurative foundations for civilizations. In brief, archaeologists divide humanity's earliest historical timeline into three ages named for the materials they used: the Stone Age (including Paleolithic, Mesolithic, and Neolithic), when the primary tool of society was stone; the Bronze Age (following a transitional "Copper Age"), which utilized bronze tools and weapons; and the Iron Age, which developed iron alloys such as steel. Each age "built" upon the technologies of its predecessor, which is why we still use stone, bronze, and iron today in what some have called the Digital Age. When all of our current virtual technologies have faded away, the cornerstones of our buildings, the cobblestones lining our streets, the granite in our kitchens, and even the tombstones over our graves will remain for our own descendants to discover and decipher.

Responsible archaeology is not about collecting the valuable objects left behind but about discovering the people who made and used them. We want to know how our ancestors lived. We want to understand what they believed about the world. We want to learn from their successes and mistakes.

The narrower field of biblical archaeology—so named because it focuses on the lands and history described in ancient Israel's writings collected in the Bible—takes the information (hopefully) objectively uncovered in the field and then uses it to contextualize and illuminate Scripture. Contrary to popular presentation, biblical archaeology does not exist to "prove" the Bible. While the distinction between *contextualizing* and *proving* may seem subtle, it should be important to the Bible reader and believer.

Holy Scripture is God-breathed. It does not require or even request that humans dig into our planet's crust to find physical evidence of its truths. It is Truth. However, that Scripture was recorded by many authors over hundreds of years at least two millennia ago. The languages, metaphors, and histories are often unknown to the modern reader and worshiper.

Many of us first encountered the Bible in Sunday school, where we were taught its stories—Adam and Eve, Moses and the Red Sea, David and the Giant, Jonah and the Whale, and so many more. I have fond memories of my own childhood Sundays, sitting and listening to my teachers or dancing and singing with my friends after enduring a long, boring sermon among adults whose height obstructed my view of the pulpit. In elementary classes, we rarely read our black-white-and-red Bible pages but often learned from colorful pamphlets and flannel board characters that easily drew our eyes and kept our attention. We were taught about the stories told in Scripture but not how to interpret Scripture itself. That had to come later, once we were fully literate and had developed analytical skills.

The problem, for me, was that the church never seemed to move beyond telling the stories to teaching exegetical techniques and historical facts. As a teenager who obeyed her youth leaders and read her Bible every day during a "quiet time," I started to notice that some of what I had been taught in Sunday school disagreed with what the Bible actually says. When I entered Rhodes College, which required all undergraduates to take theology classes, the many differences between church traditions and biblical Scripture were often the foci of our lessons, leading me to wonder whom to believe—professors who did not share my faith or beloved Sunday school teachers who had gotten the facts wrong?

My biblical archaeology studies at Harvard and subsequent digs in Israel taught me how physical artifacts can help to bridge the years between modern readers and ancient writers by filling in the details of human existence in the ancient Near East that would otherwise have been lost. They can also be "stones of help," guiding us to read Scripture as it was written, apart from the fuzzy flannel board stories that subconsciously color how we might envision the ancient world.

Bible stories, though rooted in Scripture, are often heavily influenced by the later cultures that tell them because narrative requires more description than Scripture often gives. When a verse lacks a full description, then we tend to fill in the blanks with our own experiences and understandings—unless we have somehow "seen" the ancient world. Ancient artifacts and texts reveal our ancestors and teach us how history, languages, and Scripture developed. They can also highlight just how far removed many of our traditions and narratives are from biblical truth. In the following pages, I invite you to immerse yourself in the history of the ancient Near East—the stories that the stones have heard and are ready to tell us—so you might read, study, understand, and appreciate Scripture in new yet ancient ways. You might encounter new ideas and find your long-held traditions challenged. I encourage you to examine what you were taught to believe and what you are newly learning, consider whether those ideas agree with what the biblical texts say, and be willing to change your mind or just say "I don't know" when the Bible's mysteries remain unsolved.

Beneath all this talk of ancient stones and traditional stories, remember that "no one can lay a foundation other than the one which is laid, which is Jesus Christ" (1 Cor. 3:11 NASB). We strive to better understand Scripture because we want deeper relationships with Jesus, and sometimes that means upending all we think we know so that we can recognize the true Foundation of our faith.

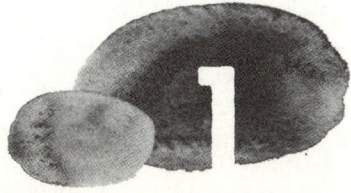

# Adam and Eve's Creation(s)

nside the Museo del Prado in Madrid, Spain, hangs a famous oil painting by Renaissance master Titian. Around 1550, he created *Adam and Eve*, his imagining of Genesis 3:6–7, which says that "when the woman saw that the tree was good for food, that it was pleasant to the eyes, and a tree desirable to make one wise, she took of its fruit and ate. She also gave to her husband with her, and he ate. Then the eyes of both of them were opened, and they knew that they were naked; and they sewed fig leaves together and made themselves coverings." Eve stands, reaching up to pick an apple from the hand of a monstrous infant with horns and two serpentine tails. Her brunette hair is long, her naked body is fair and pink, and a low branch from the apple tree covers her with foliage. To Eve's right, a tanned and hairy Adam sits, placing his fingertips gently on her shoulder as a fox glares at him. A branch from a nearby fig tree hides his nakedness from the observer.[1]

Many art historians have spent centuries analyzing the painting and asking, among other questions, why did Titian decide the "forbidden fruit" was an apple when figs are mentioned in the text? And why do Adam and Eve look and act in the ways they do? Titian and most other artists of his era had never visited the Fertile Crescent, could not read the biblical text for themselves, and were more concerned with creating beautiful works of art than accurately depicting Scripture and the ancient Near East. They painted what they knew, which were European landscapes and models that would appeal to their wealthy patrons who would enjoy seeing themselves and their homelands reflected in the masterpieces.

In spite of the inaccurate imaginings of the ancient world and Scripture itself, Renaissance works of art heavily influenced how society "sees" the text of Genesis even today. Open up any children's Bible, and the first picture is likely to be a drawing of Adam and Eve. In my own copy from the 1980s, Eve was a classic redhead sporting a fig-leaf bikini. She handed a Red Delicious apple to a brown-haired Adam in his own fig-leaf loincloth. Behind them a garter snake was coiled around a narrow tree trunk. It seems historical accuracy did not advance much in the four hundred thirty years between Titian's oil masterpieces and publishers' mass-market color prints.

Aside from the obvious errors in both depictions—Adam and Eve were probably not fair-skinned, apples are not mentioned in the text and were not indigenous to the Fertile Crescent, the fig clothes weren't crafted until *after* the fruit was consumed, and no freaky, two-tailed, horned baby-headed monsters are present in the narrative!—the first question we might should ask is, why is this the first story of creation that we teach our children when it's the second creation account in Genesis?

## *Chapter and Verse*

Have you ever been reading a passage of Scripture and thought, *That is divided in a strange place?* Maybe like me you've wondered, *Why does the story of Adam and Eve begin in Genesis 2:4 and not Genesis 2:1?* Who put the numbers into our Bible translations?

In 1227, a professor at the University of Paris and a future arch-bishop of Canterbury, Stephen Langton, divided the Latin version of the Christian Bible into chapters. His work was considered so logical that his chapter divisions were adopted not only by the Catholic Church but also by Jewish rabbis. No one was surprised that he produced such sensible and enduring work, as Langton had previously been key to the 1225 writing and passage of the Magna Carta, which ushered in modern Western democracy.[2]

About three hundred years later, a French printer named Robert Estienne gave us the verse divisions. The old joke goes that Estienne made his verse divisions while briskly riding his horse from Paris to Lyon, so any apparently stray verse number must be the result of the horse stumbling and the pen slipping. This story, though humorous, is the product of a mistranslation from Latin into French and then into English. In a letter to his son in 1551, Estienne claimed he did the work *"inter equidantum,"* which can be literally translated "on horseback" but more likely meant "while traveling" and staying at inns and homes.[3]

No horses were involved in the division of our Bible translations, but this story is a great example of how literal translations that ignore historic metaphorical meanings can foster false belief.

---

## Let's Start at the Very Beginning

I'm an astronomy lover. When I was a child, my father and I would spend brisk fall and warm summer evenings staring at the night sky. First he taught me to recognize Orion, the Big Bear, the Southern Cross (what little we could see of it from Middle Tennessee), and the Summer Triangle; then he taught me the names of the stars in those constellations. He would point at one dot of light and ask me to name it, and he loved trying to trip me up by pointing at a planet—or a satellite—instead of a star.

His at-home lessons added to and inspired what I studied in school. The summer before I started my undergraduate work, Rhodes College sent me a course catalog and forms on which to preregister for classes. At that point I "knew" I wanted to study international law, which meant a lot of introductory classes that were preselected. One of the few places I got to make a choice was in the science department. I put astronomy down as my first choice, and I got it. Thanks to a childhood spent admiring the night sky, I excelled at the labs, which mostly involved stargazing through the school's small rooftop telescopes, but I struggled with the physics- and mathematics-heavy curriculum. It turned out that astronomy is more about understanding the science behind the creation, movement, and destruction of heavenly bodies than about recognizing and utilizing pretty constellations!

My first exposure to the scientific understanding of the origins of the universe was courtesy of Carl Sagan. Most Boomer and Gen-X science enthusiasts have fond memories of Sagan's beautiful and informative series *Cosmos: A Personal Voyage* that aired on public television in 1980. (As Xennials—born on the cusp of the Gen-X and Millennial generations—my classmates and I watched *Cosmos* projected from clacking elementary school film projectors onto pull-down screens or, if we were lucky, from VCRs onto giant tube televisions.) The thirteen-episode series explained many natural phenomena from a purely scientific point of view, including the origin of life, the workings of the universe, humans' impact on the planet, and the possibility of extraterrestrial life. His work was so popular that it has been reinvented and updated for a new generation with host Neil deGrasse Tyson as *Cosmos: A Spacetime Odyssey*.

I don't watch these shows because of the worldviews of the hosts; truthfully, I watch in spite of them. Neither man shares my faith or my values—Tyson even mocks Christianity rather openly—but their scientific insights have broadened my wonder at God. They believe that the more we understand about the workings of the universe, the more obvious it is that God does not exist. I counter that the more we study science, the more obvious it is that this universe is not some happy accident full of coincidences and happenstance. The more complex and beautiful the cosmos, the more of God I see in it.

Until recently, the Big Bang theory has been the accepted scientific understanding of how the universe came into existence. It goes something like this:

> In the beginning there was nothing. No space, no time, no heat, no light. Then—literally out of nowhere—there was a "singularity." It was infinitely tiny, denser than dense, and hotter than hot. It started expanding and cooling, and light was born. We now live inside the singularity, which we call the universe.
>
> Stars, planets, and satellites started popping up about 200 million years later. Bits of matter from the singularity stuck to each other, created gravity fields, and started sucking in other bits of matter to form solid spheres. As those spheres grew and their gravity fields neared each other, all the stars, planets, and satellites started pushing and pulling against each other until they oriented themselves into galaxies and solar systems.

According to scientists, it took 13.8 billion years to get from nowhere to here, and the universe is still expanding and forming. But even the "settled science" of the Big Bang theory is changing.

The James Webb Space Telescope is a massive infrared telescope that was successfully launched on December 25, 2021. It was designed with American, Canadian, and European cooperation to study "every phase in the history of our Universe, ranging from the first luminous glows after the Big Bang, to the formation of solar systems capable of supporting life on planets like earth, to the evolution of our own Solar System,"[4] and it is sending back new data and beautiful images that are prompting scientists to reconsider long-held beliefs, mostly regarding galaxy formation.

Recent sensational headlines have stated that the telescope's data "broke the Universe,"[5] but that is not exactly true or even what most scientists are arguing in those very articles. The Big Bang theory was first suggested in 1927 by physicist and priest

Georges Lemaître. Over the next near-century, as scientists and mathematicians have learned more and built upon the writings and discoveries of their predecessors, flaws or holes in the original theory have been identified and "patched" with other theories. The images that are coming back to earth from the Webb telescope are new, and they may result in a more complete, refined scientific theory of the universe's origins because the telescope can see further back in time than its famous predecessor, the Hubble telescope, was capable of witnessing. Therefore scientists are seeing realities never before imagined, and they must investigate, evaluate, and incorporate the new evidence into the old theory. Or possibly develop an entirely new theory.[6]

In science—be it astrophysics or archaeology—our theories and conclusions are only as strong as the raw data supporting them. As it turns out, no science is ever "settled" so long as exploration is still occurring.

## How Long Is a *Day?*

Whenever I hear the Big Bang theory, I think, *That sounds a lot like what Genesis 1 describes*: Light popped out of nothing. Big stars came together, and then planets and moons did the same. The big stars started pulling the smaller planets and moons into their gravitational fields. The earth settled in next to the sun, and the moon settled in next to the earth.

That summary fits both the biblical and scientific explanations—if you ignore the time part. So how long did all this take? Was it 13.8 billion years as the scientists argue, or six days as our Bible translations state in Genesis 1:1–2:3? Let's look at the text: "God called the light *Day*, and the darkness He called Night. So the evening and the morning were the first *day*" (1:5).

The Hebrew word almost all English versions of Genesis 1 translate as "day" is *yom*. That is an accurate and common translation, but it is not the only possible translation. The word occurs approximately 2,300 times in the Bible, and it is translated as "day" in approximately two thousand of those instances. (Exact numbers depend on the Hebrew manuscripts being translated and the English versions being read.) What about the other 13 percent of the time? *Yom* can also mean an unspecified "period of time"; it can mean "year" or "era" or even just "time" in general.

## What Is Transliteration?

We all know what it means to translate: We take the meaning of a word or phrase and give it the corresponding meaning in another language. But rarely do we *transliterate* because that is only necessary when languages (such as Hebrew, Greek, Arabic, and Russian) use a different alphabet.

Let's say I wanted to understand a Spanish word. With zero knowledge of Spanish grammar or vocabulary, I could still recognize the letters and pronounce it to some degree because it uses the same Latin alphabet as English. Just speaking or hearing the word might even give me a clue as to its meaning. For example, the Spanish word *dios* translates to *god* in English. Based on the letters alone, I could guess the meaning because in English we have words such as *deity* that are obviously related to the Spanish *dios*.

But in Hebrew the word for *god* is אֱלֹהִים. Would you have any idea how to pronounce that? Without forming a deep and loving relationship with a Hebrew textbook, there is no way you could. Those don't even look like letters to the English reader, and they are written and read from right to left! So how do we make אֱלֹהִים pronounceable for the non-Hebrew speaker? We transliterate.

Each character of the Hebrew alphabet sounds like a character in the English alphabet. So instead of writing אֱלֹהִים, we write *Elohim*, substituting Latin letters for Hebrew's sounds. This helps the non-Hebrew reader "hear" the language as they read.

So how have thousands of years' worth of translators determined the accurate meaning of this and other Hebrew words that have multiple meanings? In the same way we English speakers and readers determine the meanings of words such as *date* and *watch* or any of thousands of other homonyms in our language: context.

In the context of Genesis 1, I agree with the translation of "day," but not because I think the text is describing twenty-four hours in every instance. I think "day" is correct because of the way chapter 1 is written and the shades of meaning that word has within both the English and Hebrew languages. In English, "day" can also mean an unspecified period of time, as in "back in my *day*, telephones hung on a wall!" Depending on how *yom* is used, it can have both meanings separately or simultaneously.

Moving beyond just that one word, consider Genesis 1 as a whole. It obviously doesn't flow with the rest of the book or even the rest of the Bible in style or tone. It can stand alone as a formal introduction to the anthology that is the Bible. It is an epic, awe-inspiring description of the beginning of time that highlights God's godliness. He speaks and the cosmos is created.

The chapter has a strong internal literary structure that is almost poetic in its parallels. On days one, two, and three, the great cosmic structures are formed: Light is separated from darkness, the sea is separated from the sky, and the earth emerges. On days four, five, and six, the inhabitants of those areas are made: Stars and moons populate the light and dark, creatures fill the seas and sky, and then animals and humans roam the earth. At the end of each work, God declares every part of creation "good" and each day is simply recapped by saying, "So the evening and the morning were the *n*th day."

Genesis 1 isn't a character-driven, portrait-ready story in the same way as the Adam and Eve creation story that follows it or the rest of the Genesis accounts of God's people. In Genesis 1, I see God's desire to introduce time in a way His people will understand. Here, *yom* does triple duty, not only describing the waking hours on earth but also delineating those six phases of creation and explaining why there are seven days in our weeks. As the rest of the

Bible describes—and as all of us have experienced ourselves—men and women work six days each week and rest on the seventh. God Himself is figuratively keeping the Sabbath holy (Exod. 20:8) even before the concept of "sabbath" exists. This traditional formula for work-life balance, which is heavy on the work part, seems to be waning as many of us now work from home on our computers, keep odd hours in concert with international coworkers, and worship on Saturday nights instead of Sunday mornings. But so long as our calendars show five-day weeks with two-day weekends, the connotation will stand.

Today we might call this use of *yom*—to explain why the sun rises and sets regularly and why there are seven days in a week—an *origin story*, but scholars have long called it an *etiology*. Etiologies for the creation of the universe exist in every ancient culture, but I am newly impressed every time I reread just how well Genesis describes the creation of the cosmos. Out of all creation stories across cultures, the Hebrew Bible's version is the most plausible and the only one with a chance of being supported by science. And it is millennia older than the science that agrees with it.

The Bible has tons of origin stories, especially in the book of Genesis. Obviously both creation stories are etiologies for everything in existence; Genesis 3:1–15 also explains why snakes slither on the ground instead of walking as other land creatures do or flying as seraphim do. Which brings up a good question . . .

### Which Came First—Animals or Humans?

A few years ago, I spoke to students in an upper elementary class. I told them how civilizations built on top of one another's ruins over millennia and created artificial hills filled with artifacts, how archaeologists meticulously uncover and catalog those ancient artifacts and structures, and why those activities are important to understanding the ancient world's civilizations and writings. At the end of my little presentation, I invited questions. Every hand flew up and stayed up until I heard the one question every child asks me: "Have you ever found dinosaur bones?"

I gave the simplified answer I'd always given: "Archaeologists study human civilizations, so when we reach the oldest city that was ever built in that location—beneath which there are no more buildings to excavate—we stop. Dinosaur bones would be even deeper in the ground. Paleontologists are the ones who dig up dinosaur bones." As expected, I watched my cool level drop among the students, but one child was visibly upset by what I'd said. I found out later that his parents had taught him that humans walked the earth before the dinosaurs and that Adam had named each and every -saurus from *The Land Before Time* to *Jurassic World*. By implying that dinosaurs were extinct before humans were building cities, I unintentionally rocked his ten-year-old theological world.

We will explore the dating of the earth itself more in chapter 2, but for now, let's consider how the two Genesis creation accounts are distinct from each other. Obviously their styles and tones could not be more different: Genesis 1:1–2:3 is stoic and organized, while Genesis 2:4–3:24 has an identified setting, a developed plot, multiple speaking characters, and relatable emotions. Aside from the structural differences, notice that the orders of creation seem contradictory. So why are there two versions of creation in our Bibles, and why don't they follow the same chain of events?

Linguists, theologians, and philologists who specialize in how the biblical text developed over time declare that each story had a different person writing it down for posterity.[7] The recorder of Genesis 1 had a rigid, almost scientific style that is long on process and short on details; his words make the reader wonder at the power of God more than the beauty of His creation. His brevity and repetition make the chapter easy for listeners and readers to memorize, internalize, and share. The recorder of Genesis 2–3 had a softer, more personal style that not only calls God by His name, Yahweh, but also identifies the first "male and female" mentioned in 1:27. His words draw the reader in so that we feel as if we, too, are walking in the cool garden as witnesses to our own creation, free will, and sin.

Consider our impression of God and His creation if all we had was Genesis 1. We would know that we are created in God's image, but we might have no idea what that means. He gave us one giant command:

> "Be fruitful and multiply; fill the earth and subdue it; have domin-ion over the fish of the sea, over the birds of the air, and over every living thing that moves on the earth."
>
> And God said, "See, I have given you every herb that yields seed which is on the face of all the earth, and every tree whose fruit yields seed; to you it shall be for food. Also, to every beast of the earth, to every bird of the air, and to everything that creeps on the earth, in which there is life, I have given every green herb for food." (vv. 28–30)

Those instructions are not very detailed. Genesis 1 doesn't bother to record *how* we are supposed to make more and subdue every-thing. We seem to be on our own, the final creation of a distant grand Power who made the universe and made us to take care of it and then left on a seventh-day holiday.

In the Adam and Eve narrative, we meet God as a person. He seems like any other dad who enjoys long walks in the park on cool days (3:8) and asks questions to which He already knows the answers: "Who told you that you were naked? Have you eaten from the tree of which I commanded you that you should not eat?" (3:11). He punishes misbehavior, but He cares for Adam's and Eve's physical and emotional needs throughout that punishment by clothing their now-embarrassing nakedness with warm hides instead of wilting leaves (3:21).

We need the details that come in both stories. Without Gen-esis 1, we would not know that we have been created "in God's image," and those three words actually foreshadow the events of Genesis 2–3, in which the humans try to elevate themselves from being like God to being gods themselves. (In truth, that is humanity's chief problem throughout the whole Bible and into today.) Adam and Eve also answer the question that Genesis 1 left hanging: How are we supposed to care for God's creation?

- Tend and keep the garden (2:15).
- Name (that's biblical Hebrew shorthand for "take owner-ship of") the living creatures (2:19).
- Marry (2:24).
- Bring forth children physically (3:16)—no speaking them into creation.
- Till the ground (3:23).

If God seems distant in Genesis 2:1–3, just after He makes humanity on day six, then the next story might explain why: the entrance of sin into God's creation. God spent six *yom*s (or 13.8 billion years, give or take) making perfection, and humanity went and ruined it in what seems to be a short amount of time. Their actions necessitated a fix-it mode that would require laws and sacrifices, the death of His one perfect Son, and eventually the return of His Son to reconcile humanity with Him. We simply can't imagine that level of godly frustration, and maybe that's why He gave two different sources to convey it all to us.

As an author and editor, I can imagine scribes sitting in a room with complete manuscripts of both versions. They look at them both and discuss: What's the same? What parts of these two stories can be harmonized to give us the one perfect version of creation? The answer was, nothing.

Since the scribes knew that both Genesis 1 and Genesis 2–3 were God-inspired, they included both in their entirety. No edit-ing or blending. No decision-making. God told them it was okay that Genesis 1 ordered creation as (1) plants, (2) animals, and then (3) humanity; while Genesis 2–3 ordered it as (1) man, (2) plants, (3) animals, and then (4) woman. It had to be God, because no good editor (or subsequent copyist) would have allowed such seeming contradictions to remain in any text, let alone a sacred one.

## Conclusion

Weeks before he died of a rare blood cancer on December 20, 1996, Carl Sagan wrote to Martin Gardner, a no-longer-atheist (but not Christian, either) colleague, criticizing him for suggesting there just might be one Creator God and an afterlife. Gardner responded to Sagan, "I not only think there are no proofs of God or an afterlife, I think you have all the best arguments. Indeed, I've never read anything in any of your books with which I would disagree. Where we differ is over whether the leap of faith can be justified in spite of a total lack of evidence."[8]

I think it is hard for intellectually brilliant people to make leaps of faith regardless of their vocations. Scientific fields from astrophysics and archaeology to virology and zoology are obsessed with collecting more and more and more evidence, while often declaring reasoned but personal opinions about that evidence as empirical fact. Highly analytical minds want to take everything apart, see all the pieces, and understand them. There is a certain pride that comes with perceived total understanding, and a simultaneous fear of the unknown. That combination of pride and fear too often leads scholars to belittle people of faith as weak, wrong, silly, and useless because faith is not based on evidence.

But it works the other way too. Too many Christians take pride in their complete faith in what they might call "literal" translations of Scripture, fear science that appears to contradict those translations (but more often contradicts their traditions and interpretations), and belittle scholars as weak, wrong, silly, and useless. No one trying to learn about creation is any of those things. Christians should engage with scientific discovery, be awed by God's work, and pray that everyone will see Him in the "atoms as massive as suns, and universes smaller than atoms."[9]

Most of us who believe in Intelligent Design for ourselves, for our planet, and for the cosmos have no trouble trusting the science that the sun will come up tomorrow (no matter how hard our legislatures try to alter that!), this rock will continue spinning on its axis, and time itself will continue indefinitely. It is truly a shame when readers of Genesis 1–3 miss the points of the passages while trying to discredit science with literature or Renaissance art.

God is epically powerful and wonderfully loving. He could have done anything with that so-called singularity, but He chose to make us out of nothing. It truly doesn't matter if *yom* means exactly twenty-four hours, because creation is no less amazing if it took 13.8 billion years to get us here.

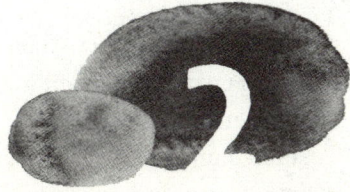

# Noah's Extraordinary Cruise

Whenever my husband David and I are traveling to Ohio along Interstate 75, we glimpse two massive evangelical landmarks that flank Cincinnati. Just thirty minutes north of the city stands a fifty-two-foot statue of Jesus called the *Lux Mundi*. It was built next to a giant pool where another more exciting statue once emerged from the water. "Big Butter Jesus" or "Touchdown Jesus," as the locals called it, was a sixty-two-foot bust of Jesus with hands raised toward heaven (or reaching toward unsuspecting motorists, depending on your perspective). It was struck by lightning and burned to its metal skeleton in 2010, but thankfully comedic songwriter Heywood Banks immortalized it in song for the world's continuing enjoyment.[1]

Thirty minutes south of Cincinnati is another more famous megastructure that has similarly tangoed with natural disaster. The Ark Encounter was built in 2016 and describes itself as "a full-size Noah's ark, built according to the dimensions given in the Bible."[2] It is actually a massive concrete and metal building that is built to look like the ark on one side—which was a good thing in 2017 and 2018 when torrential rains caused a landslide that damaged the surrounding property. This ark did not sail away and was not harmed.

A few summers back, on our way home from visiting my Amish in-laws (which is a story for another book), David and I made reservations at a pet-friendly hotel in Lexington, Kentucky, with our basset hound, Copper, so we could spend an entire day making good use of the nearly $250 we had paid for two adult tickets and parking at both the Ark Encounter and its sister attraction, the Creation Museum. It turned out that animals were more than welcome on Noah's boat but not on the grounds of these theme parks, which together support a very small zoo, camel rides, zip lines, a planetarium, a concert venue, scheduled activities, themed restaurants, and souvenir shops, most for additional fees. We certainly needed a full day to glimpse both properties, as they are forty miles away from each other—a detail that was not clear when we had bought our tickets online.

Both the Ark Encounter and the Creation Museum are outgrowths of an apologetics ministry called Answers in Genesis, which desires "to train others to develop a biblical worldview and seek to expose the bankruptcy of evolutionary ideas and their bedfellow: a '4.5 billion-year-old' earth (and an even older universe)." They go on to claim, "Where the Bible is silent or unclear, we don't pretend to know more than we know or be divisive"[3]—but that was not David's or my experience at the Ark Encounter.

The Ark Encounter and its affiliates promote a very narrow reading of the Bible called Young Earth Creationism, which states that the earth can be no older than ten thousand years and may be as young as only six thousand years, while also denigrating or simply ignoring natural evidence that it is 4.5 billion years old. Critically, they also believe there was only one ice age, which produced only one global flood in 2348 BC. Because they interpret the Bible as the "history book of the universe,"[4] they read certain English translations "literally" and use them as the foundation for any scientific understandings. In reality, most Young Earth Creationists don't completely accept every word literally; if they did, then they would still claim the earth is both flat (with "four corners" and "ends") and the center of the universe (with the sun, moon, and stars orbiting around us). Such rigid readings of Scripture began to fall away during the Enlightenment of the seventeenth and eighteenth centuries, and they were almost completely abandoned in the twentieth century as space exploration showed us images of our beautiful planet.

## How Old Is Our Planet?

On the surface, figuring the age of the earth seems easy thanks to the history described in the Old Testament. It seems all we should have to do is choose one biblical event that is corroborated in the writings of other cultures and has an accepted date, and then count backward using all the numbers stated (usually in the King James Version) for the lengths of kings' reigns and peoples' lives. To illustrate, I suggest we use the siege of Jerusalem and the Battle of Carchemish in 597 BCE, both of which are mentioned in the Bible and in the Nebuchadnezzar Chronicle.[5] From the date of those historically and archaeologically verified events, followers of Young Earth Creationism might count all the years (and months, weeks, and days) mentioned prior to 2 Kings 24:10 and add those numbers to 597, placing the year of creation at 4004 BC and the year of Noah's flood at 2348 BC.

But there is one giant problem with that methodology: It ignores the original intention of numbers as used in biblical Hebrew.

### How the Bible "Values" Numbers

*Yom* doesn't necessarily mean a "twenty-four-hour-long day," as we learned in chapter 1, and it is not the only word in biblical Hebrew with multiple meanings. Add to it the word *arbaiym*, which most English versions consistently translate as "forty." The number is first used in Genesis 7–8 to describe the length of the flood that destroyed the earth and all of its inhabitants, except for the few individuals God chose to restart life on earth: Noah's family and the animals he led onto an ark. We read that God made it rain for "forty days and forty nights" (7:12). While it is possible that water fell from the sky for exactly 960 hours, it is definitely true that Scripture is making a theological point with that number: The land was *completely* submerged under water and all living creatures were *completely* destroyed. From Genesis forward, whenever you see the word *forty* in Scripture, it has a connotation of *completion*.

When combined with the word *shaneh*, which means "years," *arbaiym shaneh* is a euphemism for a complete "generation." For example, Moses and the Hebrews roamed between Egypt and the promised land for "forty years" (Num. 32:13), or until the generation who had lived in Egypt completely died out except for God's chosen leaders, Joshua and Caleb. Kings David and Solomon each ruled "forty years" (1 Kings 2:11; 11:42). While it is possible that the men were each on the throne exactly that length of time, it is definitely true that Scripture is making a theological point with those numbers: David's and Solomon's reigns were "complete." Those men are remembered as United Israel's very best rulers, who guided a generation of Israelites toward proper worship of God and established ancient Israel as a stable, wealthy, and growing nation.

This use of numbers as shorthand is not an unusual concept in Scripture, as numbers frequently have deeper theological meanings throughout the Bible. Like the number forty, the numbers seven and twelve also have the connotation of completion—seven as the number of days of God's perfect act of creation, and twelve as the number of lunar months in a year, the number of Israel's tribes, and the number of Jesus's apostles. Three is often considered a divine number tied to the Holy Trinity. But we must guard against assuming every number mentioned in the Bible has spiritual significance. Although the early church fathers wrote about numerical symbolism, if taken too far, readers can become obsessed with numbers and treat Holy Scripture as a divining tool. God did not give us His Word to predict the future or hide some special knowledge of Himself; He gave it to us so we could glimpse holy mysteries and develop a deeper relationship with Him.

### How Scientists Date Dirt

Holding to the beliefs that the earth itself is six thousand years old and that it experienced only one ice age and only one global flood four thousand years ago requires rejection of many scientific disciplines: astrophysics, geology, paleontology, archaeology, and more. Sometimes that rejection is stated outright by Young Earth Creationists,[6] but more often, scientific discoveries, historical facts, and even theological understandings that contradict their ideas are simply ignored.

When geologists are considering the age of the earth and the weather events that shaped its crust, they have two primary tools: the ground's natural stratigraphy and a lab's radiometric dating. Inside the earth, layers of rock and sediment are stacked on top of each other by weather and magnetism. As new layers are formed on the surface, older layers are pushed down the same way buttercream spread on cake is compressed by adding layers of more cake and icing on top. Over time, as natural phenomena such as earthquakes occur, those layers can curve and buckle the way our layer cake might if it were dropped. This can be easily observed during a visit to the Grand Canyon and surrounding parks, where some of the deeper layers now appear wavy, angled, or even vertical.[7]

Earth's layers—be they smooth and horizontal or jagged and upended—each have distinctive colors, textures, and positions that can be compared to layers of similar composition at other sites. The layers' similarities tell geologists the ages of the earth's regions relative to one another. Some layers contain fossilized plant and animal materials that can also be compared and, more importantly, can be dated in a laboratory.[8]

The most commonly known radiometric dating tests carbon 14 levels in any type of organic material, from rocks to bones to fabrics to foods, and is used by geologists and archaeologists all over the world. It is imperfect, but it isn't totally useless as Young Earth Creationists sometimes claim. Beta Analytic, a major testing lab, describes radiocarbon dating this way:

> Radiocarbon, or carbon 14, is an isotope of the element carbon that is unstable and weakly radioactive. The stable isotopes are carbon 12 and carbon 13.
>
> Carbon 14 is continually being formed in the upper atmosphere by the effect of cosmic ray neutrons on nitrogen 14 atoms. It is rapidly oxidized in air to form carbon dioxide and enters the global carbon cycle.
>
> Plants and animals assimilate carbon 14 from carbon dioxide throughout their lifetimes. When they die, they stop exchanging carbon with the biosphere and their carbon 14 content then starts to decrease at a rate determined by the law of radioactive decay.
>
> Radiocarbon dating is essentially a method designed to measure residual radioactivity.[9]

By knowing how much carbon 14 is left in a sample, the age of the organism when it died can be known.

Many environmental factors can change how fast or slow an organism breaks down carbon 14, different methods of measurement may yield different results, and different labs have higher success rates than others. We are never going to be able to say, "That fossilized sea urchin died on March 15, 307 BCE," but thanks to testing and evidence in surrounding layers, we can narrow down the time of its demise to within a century.

So based on testing and observation, how long do geologists say it took for the earth to take shape and become habitable? It started out a formless clump of singularity that spun and spun with gravity into a sphere about 4.5 billion years ago. After 100 million years of that physical formation, the atmosphere (or "firmament," as Genesis calls it) settled around the globe, allowing the temperature to stabilize, gases to balance, water to condensate, and algae to grow when the earth was about 2.1 billion years old. It would be another 500 million years before the atmosphere resembled what we breathe today. During that transition, water that had covered everything began peeling back into oceans and lakes and rivers, leaving behind dry land. But of course, that dry land would not stay dry forever. Weather and waterways can cause flooding.

### When Was the Flood?

When an archaeologist is digging in the field, nothing makes her happier than finding evidence of a fire or a flood. I know that sounds morbid, but unfortunately disasters can make it easy to know when to date artifacts. They leave identifiable layers in the soil that become sandwiched between older layers of rock and newer layers of soil naturally formed by the earth's ecology and humans' activities. Thick lines of ash from raging fires or of grainy silt or sand from catastrophic floods tend to be looser in composition and different in color than the compacted earth below and above them.

Arguably the greatest disaster of all time was Noah's flood. Floods on the scale described in Genesis 6–9 leave thick layers of mud and shale that are easy to identify. Since the 1920s, teams of archaeologists and geologists have been working all over the Near East and the rest of the world with a stated or subconscious goal of finding unshakable evidence of Noah's flood. Every few years the internet screams there has been a breakthrough, only for the "discovery" to be quietly discounted a year or so later.[10] The back-and-forth is largely a product of the number of floods the ancient Near East has experienced over the last six thousand years. Many Mesopotamian sites have flood layers between 3000 and 2600 BCE, but they have all been dated to different eras of human history based on the structures and artifacts of the civilizations that surround them. Despite drilling hundreds of large core samples and excavating the civilizations that were destroyed by water, there is no evidence of a single flood that struck all of Mesopotamia at the same time, let alone the entire earth. Only regional flooding was common.

In the absence of physical geological evidence supporting Noah's voyage, I find the best witnesses for a catastrophic flood are found in the literature of ancient Near Eastern civilizations. The Sumerians and Assyrians didn't leave complete flood stories (at least, not that we've found yet), but they do divide their list of kings into "pre-flood" and "post-flood."[11] The most famous flood story, aside from the Genesis account, is in the Babylonian *Epic of Gilgamesh*. The names change, but the story is largely the same: A man and his family follow a god's instructions to save themselves (and thus humanity) from a flood. The Gilgamesh epic is itself a version of an earlier Akkadian story about a man whom the god instructs to build a round boat.

Let's compare Genesis and Gilgamesh:

So it came to pass, at the end of forty days, that Noah opened the window of the ark which he had made. Then he sent out a raven, which kept going to and fro until the waters had dried up from the earth. He also sent out from himself a dove, to see if the waters had receded from the face of the ground. But the dove found no resting place for the sole of her foot, and she returned into the ark to him, for the waters were on the face of the whole earth. So he put out his hand and took her, and drew her into the ark to himself. And he waited yet another seven days, and again he sent the dove out from the ark. Then the dove came to him in the evening, and behold, a freshly plucked olive leaf was in her mouth; and Noah knew that the waters had receded from the earth. So he waited yet another seven days and sent out the dove, which did not return again to him anymore. (Gen. 8:6–12)

> Six days and seven nights
> came the wind and flood, the storm flattening the land. . . .
> I opened a vent and fresh air (daylight!) fell upon the side of
>     my nose.
> I fell to my knees and sat weeping,
> tears streaming down the side of my nose.
> I looked around for coastlines in the expanse of the sea,
> and at twelve leagues there emerged a region (of land).
> On Mt. Nimush the boat lodged firm,
> Mt. Nimush held the boat, allowing no sway.
> One day and a second Mt. Nimush held the boat, allowing
>     no sway.
> A third day, a fourth, Mt. Nimush held the boat, allowing
>     no sway.
> A fifth day, a sixth, Mt. Nimush held the boat, allowing no
>     sway.
> When a seventh day arrived
> I sent forth a dove and released it.
> The dove went off, but came back to me;
> no perch was visible so it circled back to me.
> I sent forth a swallow and released it.
> The swallow went off, but came back to me;
> no perch was visible so it circled back to me.
> I sent forth a raven and released it.
> The raven went off, and saw the waters slither back.
> It eats, it scratches, it bobs, but does not circle back to me.[12]

These passages are the most closely related of the two texts, although the overall stories are similar. Both heroes build boats with windows and use birds to "test the waters," so to speak. Both know the flood is over when the last bird never returns. Major differences include the length of the floods, the time of the boat's landing, and the species of the test birds.

Differences in the stories come down not to historical accuracy but to literary purpose. The flood story in the *Epic of Gilgamesh* is a small part of the larger tale of how one man searches for immortality. The flood story in the Bible is a very, very small part of the larger tale of how humanity can be reconciled with God. The historical details, such as whether Noah loaded two of each animal (Gen. 7:8–9) or seven of some and two of others (7:2–3), are not as important as that overall theme.

Anyone who has ever survived a flood—be it a regional devastation as David and I experienced from our Nashville-area home in 2010, or a localized destruction due to faulty plumbing by DIY home sellers—understands the power of water. When God decides to make it rain (or a full clawfoot tub collapses over your dining room), there is no way to stop the water. It doesn't matter if a home is in a flood plain or not, when it pours for a week or a month without stopping, everything dies and everything falls. Even brick, steel, and stone structures that survive the water must be gutted so mold doesn't grow behind walls and poison the air with its spores. The annihilation is complete, and rebuilding often means moving to higher ground with firmer soils.

Floods take lives and change landscapes. That is what Genesis describes and what both geologists and archaeologists see in ancient Mesopotamia. When a site was destroyed by water or fire, survivors did not immediately rebuild. Cities would be abandoned for hundreds of years or longer, and later inhabitants were usually from different people groups. Noah's flood destroyed his world, displaced his family, and reconciled humanity to God for a short time—even if it didn't consume the globe as we see it today.

## "Giants" of Genesis

"There were giants on the earth in those days" (Gen. 6:4). For the last fifteen years, photoshopped images of men excavating giant human skeletons in India, Saudia Arabia, and New York City have floated around the internet.[13] When they resurface in our newsfeeds, it is usually thanks to a rabid group of so-called Flat Earthers who insist that all living creatures on the earth—humans, animals, and plants— were once giant in comparison to today.

The grain of that belief is in the Hebrew word *nephilim*, which only appears in Genesis 6:4 and Numbers 13:33. Its meaning is unknown, which is why many Bible translations choose (rightly, in my opinion) to transliterate the word instead of translating it. Early philologists tried to associate the root of the word to "great" or "large," but that was incorrect. The word more likely derives from a Hebrew root meaning "to fall," which is commonly used to describe warriors who "fall upon" and kill their victims. This certainly fits with the narrative context of Numbers 13, in which the Israelites fear meeting them in battle.

Those who insist that *nephilim* means "giants" might unknowingly be following a tradition started by a text called 1 Enoch, which was written between 300 BCE and 100 CE, embellishes several Genesis narratives with Greek traditions of the time, and is not regarded as Scripture by Jews or Christians. It is a fun read, but it is not history. It is an excellent example of the damage caused when we try to "fill in the blanks" of Scripture with later cultures' ideas and our own interpretations.

---

## Where Is the Ark?

If the field of archaeology has an "original sin," it is the motivations and techniques of its early practitioners. In the late nineteenth century, archaeology was largely a pastime of wealthy Europeans wanting to unearth ancient, spectacular artifacts for their own collections or for public museums that would illustrate ancient history or even "prove" the historicity of the Bible. Fun films such as 1932's *The Mummy* and 1981's *Raiders of the Lost Ark* went on to glorify archaeology as a swashbuckler's dream job, filled with adventure and free of the red tape that comes with objective scientific research. While archaeology has Indiana Jones to thank for inspiring many of today's excavators to join the profession, it can also blame him for encouraging the idea that archaeologists are mere grave robbers and fortune hunters who need only ride a motorcycle, hold onto a brimmed hat, and follow obscure signs from questionable sources.

Rarely a week goes by when someone doesn't ask me if Noah's ark has been found. Genesis 8:4 tells us it rested "on the mountains of Ararat," but that isn't exactly a GPS locator. The identification of Ararat as a region within modern-day Turkey came during the Middle Ages and was quickly adopted by the Armenian Apostolic Church, whose Etchmiadzin Cathedral claims to have held a piece of the ark since the fourth century.[14]

Wild stories about the discovery of the giant artifact have been around for centuries, but the most famous claim was made by *Life* magazine in 1960 on behalf of Turkish soldiers and an un-identified "expedition including American scientists" who "on a mountain 20 miles south of Mt. Ararat" saw "a boat-shaped form about 500 feet long."[15] This short article motivated one of the most outspoken pseudoarchaeologists of our time—a nurse anesthetist named Ron Wyatt, who had zero scientific training, archaeological education, or legal permits—to devote his life to (often illegally) exploring the Near East in search of Noah's ark, the ark of the covenant, Sodom and Gomorrah, and evidence of the exodus, all of which he claimed to have found before his death in 1999.[16] He found none of those things, not even a splinter from Noah's ark.

As I have stated, all theories should be held lightly so long as exploration is still occurring. That includes any statement that claims "absence of evidence is evidence of absence." It is possible that Noah's ark will be found in a petrified state one day, but it is unlikely for two reasons. The simplest reason is that wood rarely survives for hundreds or thousands of years, even in an arid climate—let alone on a snow-capped volcano with warm dry summers and cold wet winters. When three-thousand-year-old

buildings are excavated in Israel, the wood posts that upheld second stories are long gone; we identify them by the remaining post
holes they were placed in and the microscopic fragments decompo-
sition sometimes leaves behind. Wood simply does not survive
that long.

But the likeliest reason we will never find this ark is that its passengers would have reused it for parts. According to the Genesis
account, Noah and his family stepped out of the ark into a brand-
new world with no shelter. They had wild animals with them who
might have wandered away, but the domesticated animals onboard
would have needed homes—as would the humans! In their new,
high-altitude home, with a promise that God would never again
destroy the earth with a flood, there was no good reason to keep
the ark as it was. The men and women would have had no interest
in preserving it for future generations when they had immediate
physical needs to meet.

## Conclusion

One of the first lessons I was taught as a budding archaeologist
was this: "If you look for it, then you'll find it." I heard this from
my graduate adviser and Ashkelon dig director, Lawrence Stager,
in reference to excavations. He meant that if you go to a site expecting to find something, such as evidence of a flood or the remnants of Noah's ark, then your desire to be right will bias your
interpretation of the raw data in front of you. You will "not see"
evidence that disproves your theory, and you might overinflate or
misinterpret evidence that would support it. This is absolutely true
in archaeology, and it is evidenced every few years when someone
loudly proclaims the discovery of a spectacular artifact that will
supposedly change the world but only enriches the announcer and
is quickly but quietly proven wrong.

That sentiment applies to more than just scientific discovery.
Objectivity barely exists today, as advertising and algorithms work

to reinforce what we each already believe. Simply compare the home pages of your favorite and your most hated news sources. They no longer just spin stories to advocate a certain viewpoint; they only share stories that inherently support what they think their readers and viewers want to see. And now that artificial intelligence is aggressively tracking all we do on our smart devices, the technology ensures we are only given what we already like because that keeps us scrolling (and viewing ads that pay the news sites). The less we purposefully search for truth outside of our usual sources, the fewer facts we see.

In a world where individuals' opinions are now treated as "their truths," the best way to distinguish actual truth from fiction might be to follow the money—ad generated or otherwise. In modern archaeology, the workers are volunteers who pay their own travel expenses, and the dig directors are university professors with teachers' salaries. The excavations themselves are funded by donors and grants, but there is never enough money. The funds must pay for state-of-the-art technology that makes the digs efficient and the data accurate, while hand tools and sunshades are decades old and deteriorating, everyone shares a bedroom with at least two other volunteers for eight weeks, and there is no guarantee that a summer's sweat and sacrifices will yield results. The job is not lucrative, and most of us who invest our lives in collecting data, studying artifacts, and sharing findings do so for the love of history and people—not for fame or fortune or even fun.

After returning home from the Ark Encounter, where I was told at every turn that centuries' worth of labors by scientists, theologians, and linguists were "bankrupt," I wondered what it would cost to visit the British Museum today. I first visited it when I was seventeen, and I still remember the queues of people waiting to see the Rosetta Stone, which unlocked the translation of ancient Egypt's languages and history, the halls of Assyrian reliefs and tablets of Mesopotamian Chronicles that illustrate and describe wars mentioned in 1 and 2 Kings, and even an early manuscript of the *Epic of Gilgamesh*. Surely tickets to such a place to see actual history would exceed the $250 that David and I paid for the bare-minimum tours of reproductions and reimaginings at a theme park in Kentucky?

Admission to the British Museum is free.

# Father Abraham's Many Sons

One morning in the spring of 1989, I pranced into my elementary Sunday school class wearing a hand-me-down pink-and-white sailor dress and too-small white tights with saddle shoes. I loved that dress because it was pink—which looked terrible with my wild red hair—and because it twirled. We children had all been sitting more or less quietly in preaching service for the last hour, so we needed to move. Our teachers put in a cassette recording of "Father Abraham," and we began to sing and dance:

> Father Abraham had many sons,
> Many sons had Father Abraham.
> I am one of them, and so are you.
> So let's just praise the Lord! Right arm!

We swung our right arms as one might do when marching. Each time we repeated the verse, we added another motion: swinging our left arms, stomping our right and left feet, and nodding our chins up and down. At the end we sang, "Turn around, sit down!"

which I did with a flourish befitting my twirly skirt. Up my skirt soared as down my tights rolled. My face flushed the color of my hair, and I swore off pantyhose then and for the rest of time.

The soundtrack for this most embarrassing story is a song written by a Dutch lyricist and children's performer named Pierre Kartner and recorded in 1973.[1] It was so popular that he took on the stage name *Vader* [Father] *Abraham* and performed the song wearing a fake beard until he could grow out his own.[2]

Somewhere between 1970s Netherlands and 1980s America, the lyrics changed. Kartner had written,

> Father Abraham had seven sons,
> Seven sons had Father Abraham.
> And they never laughed, and they didn't cry.
> All they did was go like this: right arm!

If Kartner ever explained his lyrics to audiences or media, then the exegesis has been lost to history. But a surface reading seems to agree with the biblical text. Abraham did indeed have seven sons: Ishmael by Hagar, Isaac by Sarah, and five others by Keturah. (Keturah's sixth child, Shuah, was likely a daughter.) The description of their stoicism—neither laughing nor crying—is not scriptural and probably reflects the intended outcome of the song, that the children will tire themselves out with the motions and then politely sit and listen to their teachers.

Another darker possibility exists as the inspiration for the song. Kartner was raised Catholic, and he may have grown up hearing the story of the seven Jewish brothers and their mother who were martyred by Antiochus IV Epiphanes for not accepting Greek traditions that violated Jewish laws. The story is recorded in 2 Maccabees 7, a historical book (which we will explore more in chapter 10) within the Catholic canon but not the Hebrew Bible or Protestant canon. The men's tongues, scalps, hands, and feet were cut off before their still-living bodies were cooked in a massive frying pan. Without tongues, they could not laugh or cry out. As hands and feet were removed, the limbs may have flailed. If Kartner had this story in mind as he wrote, then the song is more like the nursery rhyme "Mary, Mary, Quite Contrary"—which describes the atrocities of Queen "Bloody" Mary I of England who tortured, killed, and buried Protestant "pretty maids all in a row"—than any traditional hymn or praise chorus.

No matter the exact inspiration, the "many sons" version of the song that I learned has deeper theological implications for Christians than the original Dutch lyrics, echoing Paul's words in Galatians 3:29: "If you are Christ's, then you are Abraham's seed, and heirs according to the promise." Changing the lyrics means children not only get their wiggles out, but they also learn their place in God's family ("I am one of them, and so are you") and the importance of actively worshiping God in a corporate setting ("so let's just praise the Lord"). Did I understand how Gentiles were metaphorically grafted into God's family by the work of Jesus in third-grade Sunday school? Of course not. But the song laid a foundation that I would remember and build upon in adulthood, which remains the goal of children's Bible teachers today.

As adults, we can move beyond the earworm that is "Father Abraham" and consider the man's place in Scripture. Abraham was a ninth-great-grandson of Noah, and genealogically speaking, he had no standing when God first spoke to him. He wasn't the wealthy firstborn of firstborns, he had no children, he wasn't living in the future promised land, and he probably worshiped the gods of Ur. He was an unlikely choice to father all of God's people, and even after he encountered God, his life was far from perfect. But God has the habit of choosing the least likely people to be His heroes.

## Noah's Many Sons

After the flood left only Noah and his family to repopulate the earth, we read that his descendants lived exceedingly long lives and began to build cities. In Genesis 11, the people in Mesopotamia's land of Shinar formed and baked bricks and attempted to erect a tower that could reach the heavens, presumably so they could become gods themselves. God responded by "confusing" the peoples' languages and spreading them throughout the known world. The site of the tower was then known as Babel (which means "confusion") and later Babylon. In this one origin story, we learn how Babylon got its name and wicked reputation, why different languages exist, and how ancient and enduring human hubris is! These people wanted to "make a name" for themselves (v. 4) rather than follow God's instructions to "be fruitful and multiply" and "bring forth abundantly in the earth and multiply in it" (9:7).

It seems the descendants of Noah's son Ham were the ones living in the land of Shinar and building Earth's first skyscraper. From the so-called Table of Nations in Genesis 10, we learn both the names of Noah's descendants and the areas where they eventually settled. The names do double duty as personal names and geographical names. Sometimes they are transliterated, and sometimes they are translated. Consider Ham's son Mizraim, first mentioned in Genesis 10:6 alongside his brothers Cush, Put, and Canaan. Later in the Bible, Mizraim (and sometimes Cush and Put, too) gets translated to a place name you'll recognize: Egypt (and Ethiopia and Libya, respectively).

Genesis 10's extensive genealogy is not just the ancient equivalent of Ancestry.com; it serves a greater theological purpose, as do all biblical genealogies. This one shows how all people all over the world come from the same ancestor, Noah, through his three sons, Ham, Japheth, and Shem. The genealogy then subtly foreshadows the coming tensions between some of those people groups as the history of ancient Israel later unfolds in the Bible. Ham's descendants are easily recognized by ancient and modern readers because many would become the first empire builders around the Mediterranean, including Egypt, Ethiopia, Sheba, Philistia, and Canaan. Japheth's descendants are harder to identify, as they don't often appear in the rest of the Bible or in texts from other cultures. Based on the noncanonical Book of Jubilees (which is a first-century-BCE retelling of Genesis, not unlike the Book of Enoch), Japheth's descendants would be the later empire builders of Europe and Asia, north of the ancient Near East. They are traditionally—although not scripturally—associated with the Celts, Scythians, Medes, and Greeks.[3]

After the Babel incident, the biblical genealogist focuses on a single branch of Noah's family: the children of Shem who would become the Hebrew and Arab peoples known as *Semites*. As generations of Noah's children grew up and moved apart, the cousins became sometimes distant neighbors and frequent enemies. From Shem's children come the Elamites, Assyrians, and Arameans; further down his line are the Moabites, Ammonites, and of course, the Israelites, Edomites, Ishmaelites, and Midianites, among so many others who settled between modern-day Iran and the Mediterranean Sea.

### Where and When Was Abram?

Nine generations after Shem, a man named Abram lived in "Ur of the Chaldeans" (Gen. 11:28), where he married a woman named Sarai who "was barren" and "had no child" (v. 30). After the death of his brother Haran, Abram and his family traveled from Ur toward Canaan and stopped in a city also called Haran (where, based on the names, we assume the brother had been a founder and elder). In Haran, the family settled, Abram's father died, and Abram heard his first message from God: "Leave your home and family in Haran, and go to an unspecified location that I will show you. Then I will bless you and all of your descendants" (12:1–3, paraphrased). Abram and Sarai then continued on their journey, eventually making a life for themselves within Canaan. At the end of his life, Abraham sent a servant back to his "country and to

[his] kindred" of "Aram-naharaim, to the city of Nahor" (24:4, 10 NRSV) to find a wife for his son Isaac.

For the last one hundred years, two sites have been proposed as the physical location for Abram's first hometown of Ur. Based solely on the biblical text, everyone thought until the twentieth century that Ur was located in southern Turkey near today's Syrian border. The city of Urfa and the region around it have been inhabited since 9000 BCE, and local tradition still maintains it was Abram's home. Only thirty miles from Urfa is the city of Haran, which is ten miles north of the Syrian border, retains that name even today, was a major city during the Middle Bronze Age, and would have been on a major road between Canaan and Urfa.[4]

That reasonable identification of Urfa as Abraham's Ur was challenged in the 1920s and 1930s as British archaeologist Sir Leonard Woolley excavated another city called Ur, this one about one thousand miles from Haran at Tell el-Muqayyar in southern Iraq, following the discovery and translation of cuneiform-inscribed bricks and cylinders buried within buildings' foundations. The writings stated that the city was called Ur, as were several others in antiquity. The excavations revealed a large port city that had been home to wealthy residents for thousands of years, as well as Sumerian queen Puabi, whose opulent burial laden with gold and jewels dated to approximately 2600 BCE. In his descriptions of the city, Woolley sensationally identified it as "the biblical home of Abraham,"[5] and as the spectacular artifacts made it back to the British Museum and the University of Pennsylvania Museum of Archaeology and Anthropology, the public was wowed and did not question his claims.

Determining which is the correct site of biblical Ur is impossible with the information we currently have. Woolley did not find an "Abraham was here" inscription, and excavators at Urfa or Haran likely would not either. The sites in and around Haran need to be thoroughly excavated, but that is unlikely to happen considering the current political climate within and around Syria.

Unfortunately, it is just as difficult to date Abraham as it is to locate his homes and travels since the events described in Genesis do not have contemporary parallels in other cultures. Theologians' estimates for when Abraham, Isaac, Jacob, and Jacob's sons lived range from 2000 BCE to 1500 BCE, which is inexact but does fit within Near Eastern archaeologists' designation of the Middle Bronze Age, 1950–1539 BCE. Until extrabiblical evidence is found, all archaeologists can do (or ever should do) is excavate sites throughout the region to better understand how life was lived by the cities' inhabitants. By understanding the cultures that surrounded the patriarchs and matriarchs, we can better understand the people and texts themselves.

## What Is BCE?

So much of archaeological work is about dating the ancient world. We want to know when civilizations rose and fell, what they traded, and how they warred with each other because it helps us to understand cultural development. Establishing universal timelines is challenging because every culture throughout history has had its own system of dating. Today most of the world follows the Gregorian calendar, named for Pope Gregory XIII who instituted it in 1582, which is astronomically accurate but can be difficult to harmonize with other ancient calendars.

Here are three facts everyone should know about our modern world's dating system:

1. There was no Year 0, so each millennium (and century and decade) begins on a 1. This means that the twenty-first century wasn't ushered in by the Y2K scare; it started January 1, 2001.

2. The years prior to nonexistent Year 0 are counted backward in time, and beginning in the eighth century with the writings of the Venerable Bede, they were followed by the designation BC (meaning "before Christ"). The years after nonexistent Year 0 count forward and were *preceded* by the designation AD (meaning *anno domini*, "in the year of our Lord"). The use of

BC and AD was not widely known until Holy Roman Emperor Charlemagne mandated it for government documents in AD 801, and it took another six hundred years to become common outside of official papers.

3. The shift from BC and AD to BCE ("before the common era") and CE ("common era") began with Johannes Kepler in the seventeenth century and was largely adopted by Jews in the nineteenth century. It became standard for academics in many fields and for most writing style guides during the twentieth century because it is considered a neutral dating system that does not rely on the traditions of one region or one religion.

When I first learned about BCE and CE in my undergraduate Bible classes, I thought that the world was trying to get rid of Christ. While there might be some truth to that statement in some situations, I agree that the new date designations are more sensible. Biblical archaeology ends prior to the birth of Jesus (when classical archaeology picks up), and it involves many ancient cultures that had their own dating systems and theological traditions. Note that most archaeologists in Israel are Jewish, but we don't follow the Jewish calendar either because it, too, would be confusing for Assyriologists and Egyptologists in adjacent nations whose work dovetails with that of biblical archaeologists.

For Christians, the more important reason we should consider moving past the nonbiblical, medieval-government-imposed tradition of BC and AD is that Jesus probably wasn't born in AD 1. Considering scriptural, historical, literary, and archaeological evidences, the year 4 BC (or maybe even a bit earlier) is a better fit for His birthday. It is far less confusing if Jesus was born "before the common era" than "before Christ," as that second designation would instigate all sorts of theological conundrums![6]

## City Life During the Middle Bronze Age

The Tower of Babel narrative in Genesis 11 is a curious, short account of one people group trying to make themselves gods, as did

Adam and Eve. But one little word always catches my attention in verse 3, because it is the first mention of man-made construction materials: *bricks*. Noah honed wood for his ark, and stones had long been used (and reused) to build walls. But mudbricks were a technology that required trial and error to develop and time to create.

To date, the earliest mudbricks in the world have been found at Tel Jericho and have been dated to 9000 BCE.[7] The makers would stir together soil, water, and a binder—often wheat chaff—and form the bricks with their hands. The bricks would then be laid in the sun to dry. Eventually, the process was "automated" as people invented molds to keep the bricks uniform and speed their creation. By 5000 BCE, some locations were baking the bricks, making them more durable. Finished bricks would then be laid with more mud as mortar, often on top of short stone foundations.[8]

Over time, weather could damage the bricks. Unfired bricks might melt and curve as repeated rain events softened the bricks or earthquakes made them ripple. But sometimes, if a city was the victim of fire-wielding attackers, the heat of the destruction would bake the bricks in place, making them easier to excavate thousands of years later.

Throughout the Mesopotamian cultures of Sumer, Assyria, and Babylonia between 2200 and 500 BCE, ziggurats were built for religious purposes in major cities. They would be stepped, pyramidal structures with sun-dried mudbrick interiors and baked mudbrick facades. There were no chambers inside, and the towers would be ascended by exterior staircases. It is thought that this is what Ham's children were building at Babel. The best-preserved ziggurat in the world is at Sir Leonard Woolley's Sumerian Ur (c. 2000 BCE), but the most famous is the Etemenanki ziggurat associated with the temple of Marduk. Etemenanki was at least six hundred years newer than Ur's, was built by the Neo-Assyrians when they had control of the city of Babylon, and was destroyed by Sennacherib in 689 BCE. Only its foundations remain, while

Sumerian Ur's ziggurat was restored by Neo-Babylonian king Nabonidus in the 550s BCE and again by Saddam Hussein in the 1980s CE.

Without much knowledge of archaeology or ancient Near Eastern history, I always imagined Abram and his family roaming around a dusty dry wilderness with their flocks and herds, popping up tents overnight, and occasionally running into heavenly messengers and local kings. In reality, the regions of Sumer, Canaan, and Egypt were mostly fertile and had been dotted by walled cities with thousands of residents worshiping various gods and goddesses for hundreds of years by the time Abram's caravan was passing through and moving in.

If you ever visit one of the countries forming the geographical region called the Levant—be it Israel, Jordan, Syria, Lebanon, Cyprus, or southern regions of Turkey—you might scan the horizon and see many lonely looking hills. Each of these unnatural mounds is called a *tel* (or *tell* or *tall*, depending on the language being transliterated), which means "mound." With names like that, it is obvious that archaeologists are more concerned with being factual than creative!

Once humans developed farming techniques and no longer needed to move constantly to hunt and gather all of their food, they began to build permanent settlements near waterways and major roads with good sight lines in case any animal or human enemies might attack. Early homes were built close to each other, had round footprints, and were constructed of stone. When those structures were abandoned for any number of reasons—such as natural disaster, enemy invasion, or widespread illness—the earth would reclaim the site. Erosion and weather would cause dirt and grass to cover the structures until another people group came in hundreds of years later. Attracted by the same access to water, trade, and defense, this second group would build again. As they dug down for their own buildings' foundations, they inevitably found stones from the previous occupants that would be reused in the new city's walls. The walls themselves might be stone, or they might be built with mudbricks that could be made in any quantity and built to taller heights. When tragedy struck that second civilization, the cycle would begin again: earth covering over the structures, time passing, another group liking the site's location, and construction commencing—the new inhabitants again reusing what was in the earth below and adding their own technologies to the new structures above.

As people built upon unknown numbers of civilizations beneath their feet, the tel developed. With the weight of the earth and structures above them, the lowest layers would compress, sometimes spread, and the edges would slope down. Today, when archaeologists choose a tel to excavate, they number the layers of civilization from the top down. The surface of the tel, with all its grass and modern uses, is level one. The bottom of the tel—the first civilization to build in that location—has the highest number. Each of those levels is distinguished from the others by color and texture, and if earthquakes hit, then the layers would become wavy instead of straight. Does this sound familiar? It is because tel development mimics the earth's own layers, and both geologists and archaeologists call their layers *strata*.

One of the best examples of a tel is at Megiddo. The fifteen-acre site was almost continuously occupied between 5000 and 350 BCE and has twenty strata. It sits sixty meters above the surrounding Jezreel Valley in Israel and on the trade line that ran between Egypt, Anatolia, and Mesopotamia.[9] From the top of the city, it was easy to see the invaders or caravans who might be approaching, which explains why Megiddo is the site of the world's first recorded battle and is likely the site of its penultimate Battle of Armageddon.[10] Megiddo has been well excavated, beginning in 1925 and only closing down during wartime. The first excavation was conducted by the University of Chicago's Institute of Oriental Research and funded by John Rockefeller. Yigael Yadin worked there on behalf of Hebrew University between 1960 and

1971, and since 1992, Israel Finkelstein and David Ussishkin have led Tel Aviv University's teams.

Cities within such tels have shown us that during the Middle Bronze Age, people lived inside their city walls, but their herds and fields remained outside. As Abram and his family were moving throughout Canaan—around the cities of Shechem (Gen. 12:6), Bethel and Ai (12:8), Hebron (13:18), Dan (14:14), Gerar (20:1), and Beersheba (22:19)—they would not necessarily have had to enter any city to meet the inhabitants. But when business needed to be conducted, it would have happened at the city gate. Excavators at Tel Dan recently restored and protected the world's oldest arched gate. Popularly known as Abraham's Gate, it has basalt stone foundations topped with mudbricks and was built c. 1750 BCE to protect the Canaanite city that was then called Laish.[11]

Genesis 23 tells the story of how Abraham legally acquired his first piece of land at one such city gate. His wife Sarah had died in the vicinity of Hebron, and he needed a place to bury her and their descendants. He haggled a bit with the owners, wanting to pay full price for property they were ready to give to him for free, but eventually "the field of Ephron which was in Machpelah, which was before Mamre, the field and the cave which was in it, and all the trees that were in the field, which were within all the surrounding borders, were deeded to Abraham as a possession in the presence of the sons of Heth, before all who went in at the gate of his city" (vv. 17–18).

According to Genesis, the Cave of Machpelah holds the bones of Sarah and Abraham (23:19; 25:9), Isaac and Rebekah, and Jacob and Leah (49:29–31). Jewish tradition adds the idea that inside the Cave of Machpelah is the ancient entrance to Eden, where Adam buried Eve and was later buried himself. It also claims that Esau sold his right to be buried in the cave, that he was decapitated by one of Joseph's grandsons during an argument over the property, and that his head rolled into dead Isaac's lap where it remains. Muslim tradition states that Joseph was also buried at the Cave of

Machpelah in Hebron, not in Shechem as the Bible claims (Josh. 24:32).[12]

Paying the full four hundred shekels of silver for this large piece of property was important to Abraham so that the land could not be reclaimed from him or his family in the future. But where did he get the money? There is nothing in the earlier chapters of Abram's story to indicate that he came from a wealthy family; he had to build his own wealth, and some of that came from the spoils of his battles while the rest came to him in a morally questionable manner.

## Abraham's Material Blessings

There are three similar stories in Genesis 12, 20, and 26. Theologians refer to them as the "wife-sister narratives," and they are called *doublets* (even though there are three of them) because they seem to be telling the same story—with different details—multiple times. Another excellent example of a doublet is seen within the Noah's ark account. As Noah was loading the ark, we read that he prepared for "seven each of every clean animal, a male and his female; two each of animals that are unclean, a male and his female, also seven each of birds of the air, male and female" (Gen. 7:2–3). But we are also told the passengers "of clean animals, of animals that are unclean, of birds, and of everything that creeps on the earth" boarded "two by two" (7:8–9). All versions of doublets were preserved in Scripture because the scribes didn't choose which was right and which was wrong; we are left to consider the meanings behind the details and what they reveal about God.

In the wife-sister narratives, Abraham and Isaac try to pass off Sarah and Rebekah as their sisters because the men fear they will be killed by foreign leaders who want to marry their beautiful wives.

In the first story, Abram and Sarai have immigrated to Egypt to avoid a famine in Canaan. He tells an unnamed pharaoh that she is his sister, and she ends up marrying the pharaoh while Abram

57

is showered with expensive gifts: "The woman was taken to Pharaoh's house. He treated Abram well for her sake. He had sheep, oxen, male donkeys, male and female servants, female donkeys, and camels" (12:15–16). Except for the messy detail that Abram and Sarai were married, this would have been a common marriage contract. The pharaoh gave all the gifts to Abram as the bride price to "buy" Sarai. It is not clear if "taken to Pharaoh's house" means she was part of his harem or became a wife of royal standing, but either way the implication is that they slept together. The fact that God later sent plagues underscores this, since adultery would have been the pharaoh's only crime in this situation.

One time wasn't enough for old Abraham (and by now he was old)! After he left Egypt—and after he made his name-changing covenant with God (Gen. 17)—Abraham pulled the same con and married Sarah off to the unnamed king of Gerar, a Canaanite city between Gaza and Beersheba, who also gave him "sheep, oxen, and male and female servants" and "a thousand pieces of silver" (20:14, 16). Isaac must have heard those stories from his parents, because in Genesis 26 he did exactly the same thing with his wife, Rebekah, also in Gerar with a king named Abimelech (who may or may not have been the same man who married Sarah).

The stories themselves don't have much moral value, except maybe to remind men not to lie about their relationships with their wives, but they do have redemptive value. These people were all liars and possibly adulterers. In the micro, God saved them from the situations they caused themselves and allowed them to accumulate wealth and countless descendants. In the macro, Abraham, Sarah, and Isaac managed to make it into the so-called Hall of Faith:

By faith Abraham obeyed when he was called to go out to the place which he would receive as an inheritance. And he went out, not knowing where he was going. By faith he dwelt in the land of promise as in a foreign country, dwelling in tents with Isaac and

Jacob, the heirs with him of the same promise; for he waited for the city which has foundations, whose builder and maker is God.

By faith Sarah herself also received strength to conceive seed, and she bore a child when she was past the age, because she judged Him faithful who had promised. Therefore from one man, and him as good as dead, were born as many as the stars of the sky in multitude—innumerable as the sand which is by the seashore. (Heb. 11:8–12)

They are among the Bible's greatest heroes, in spite of what they did wrong. That is a fact all of Abraham's children—genetic or adopted—should celebrate in triplicate.

## Conclusion

Exactly thirty years after my Sunday school wardrobe malfunction, I had the opportunity to visit Father Abraham (and at least one of his sons) at his burial site in Hebron. The Cave of Machpelah has been covered by the Tomb of the Patriarchs and Matriarchs since the first century, when Herod the Great constructed the building as a synagogue. It has functioned as a worship center ever since, switching between synagogue, mosque, church, and back again. It has been repaired and renovated and expanded and divided many times in the last two thousand years, and it is the only building on the earth to have continuously functioned for that long—thanks to stone foundation walls that are six feet thick.

Since a terrorist attack in 1994, the tomb has been divided down the middle (mosque in the east and synagogue in the west). The Jews and Muslims each have complete access to the entire building on their ten holiest days each year, and when holy days overlap, each religion gets the whole building for twelve hours. That division extends beyond the building and into Hebron itself, leaving 20 percent of the city for Israelis and 80 percent for Palestinians. Neither group can cross into the side of the city that is not theirs;

only foreigners who are neither Jewish nor Muslim are allowed across the heavily armed checkpoints.

As an American Christian, I was able to visit both sides of the city and both sides of the building. On the mosque side, I was given a hooded cape to cover myself (no twirly skirts or rolling pantyhose would be tolerated!); on the synagogue side, the men were given yarmulkes to cover their heads. One of the first things I noticed was that the monuments inside the building honoring the men and women buried in the cave beneath our feet were also divided: The Muslims get Isaac and Rebekah, and the Jews get Jacob and Leah. Sadly, Abraham and Sarah's monuments are split in two—half in the mosque and half in the synagogue.

We tend to think of Abraham as the grandfather of the twelve tribes, but he was so much more. Obviously, Muslims count him as "father" as they came through the descendants of his firstborn son, Ishmael. But he is also the father of the Edomites and Moabites, who would wage many wars against David and the Israelites. And critically, he's the father of the Midianites, who sold Abraham's great-grandson Joseph into Egyptian slavery but later introduced the worship of Yahweh to Moses.

Gentiles must look outside of the Bible's genealogies to see Abraham as father. Popular DNA tests are surprising more and more people with the knowledge they may have a drop of Abraham's blood inside them, but not all and not me. As a Christian of northern European descent, I have been adopted into God's family, and for that I praise the Lord.

# Joseph's Fall and Rise

Nestled among Nashville's gray downtown government buildings sits the sparkling Tennessee Performing Arts Center. Each year since 1980, big-budget traveling shows have visited the venue's grand Jackson Hall, allowing locals to witness incomparable actors such as Carol Channing in her title role of *Hello, Dolly!* and to feel the Palais Garnier's chandelier crash to the stage during *Phantom of the Opera*. In 1995, my parents took me to see *Joseph and the Amazing Technicolor Dreamcoat*. Although I don't remember it being my favorite production, the song "Close Every Door" stuck with me; years later I would sing it in my first jury at Rhodes College.

The show was first developed in 1967, when Andrew Lloyd Webber was approached by a friend to write a pop cantata for a middle-school boys' choir to perform at their Easter concert in London. He asked his friend Tim Rice to collaborate on a topic and write the lyrics. The twenty-minute special grew into a full musical in 1973, after Webber and Rice had success with *Jesus Christ Superstar*.[1] It has been running for over fifty years and has become a popular production for schools, as it naturally involves a choir of children and is short by musical standards. Audiences can still feel its late 1960s roots in the music and costumes. *Joseph* has no spoken words, and each song is from a different genre: Country, gospel, rock and roll, reggae, and even a Parisian Apache (pronounced ah-PASH) dance make for an ever-surprising evening that manages to tell Joseph's story in less time than it takes to read Genesis 37–50.

The show has not always been viewed as the child-friendly production its creators intended. In 2017, a New Zealand community performed the show for all the schools around the nation's capital, and someone changed the lyrics to "Close Every Door." Instead of ending it with "Children of Israel are never alone," the actors sang "children of kindness are never alone." This did not sit well with Rice and Webber, who both responded that the edit was unauthorized and was a sloppy attempt at political correctness. "That song is a serious moment and a key point in the show," said Webber. "It is about the connection Joseph suddenly makes with Israel. Tim was paraphrasing the Bible and it should be kept that way."[2]

Like many of Andrew Lloyd Webber's musicals, *Joseph* is a product of its time. Were it written today, I wonder if the Egyptian slaves would be go-go dancers, if the pharaoh would be an Elvis-like character, or if that coat would be "Technicolor" or simply have long sleeves.

## Joseph's Early Life in Canaan

No offense to Webber and Rice—or to almost every children's Bible on the market—but Joseph's amazing coat probably wasn't made of many colors.

In Genesis 37:3 we read that Jacob had given his seventeen-year-old favorite son, Joseph, a tunic that was *pasim*. This Hebrew word only occurs twice in the Bible, so its translation is uncertain. It seems to be related to an Aramaic word that means "palms of hands / soles of feet," or it might be related to an Akkadian word for a ceremonial gold-trimmed robe. The most likely translation is "long-sleeved," as in, the fabric reached the wearer's palms and maybe his feet too. There is little chance the word has anything to do with pigmentation.

So why do most of our English translations of the Bible read "many-colored" when we know that is wrong? Tradition. The first translation of the Hebrew Scriptures was created in the third century BCE. It was a Greek translation known as the Septuagint, and it translated *pasim* as "many-colored" for no apparent reason. Subsequent translations, including the fourth-century-CE Latin Vulgate and the seventeenth-century English King James Version, followed the Septuagint's lead even though it was incorrect. (A similar thing happened with the name "Red Sea," which we will "dive" into in the next chapter.)

No matter if the tunic was dyed many colors, embroidered with gilded thread, or simply a cover-all, its construction was costly. Such a gift to a younger son tangibly indicated Jacob's favoritism of Joseph over his ten older brothers: Reuben, Simeon, Levi, Judah, Dan, Naphtali, Gad, Asher, Issachar, and Zebulun. This kind of preferential treatment of the non-heir was countercultural, and clearly it and Joseph's sassiness pushed the older brothers to eliminate him.

I have to wonder why Jacob openly played favorites and sewed discord among his sons, and why Joseph was the object of his affection. The answer may simply be that Jacob loved Joseph's mother, Rachel, more than his other wife, Leah, and his two concubines, Bilhah and Zilpah.

As I was taught the story of Genesis 29–31 in Sunday school, Jacob fell into love at first sight with his beautiful cousin Rachel, the younger daughter of his maternal uncle Laban. Laban had an older daughter, Leah, who was ugly and mean. Jacob labored seven years for Laban to pay Rachel's bride price, but at the wedding, Laban switched his daughters so that Jacob would unknowingly marry Leah. After a weeklong "honeymoon," Jacob then married Rachel "on credit," immediately taking her as his second wife and agreeing to work for Laban another seven years. Shenanigans ensued between the sisters, as Leah easily had four children while Rachel had none. The women fought over their alone time with Jacob, and they used their maids as surrogate mothers (as Sarai had used Hagar in Gen. 16) to have more sons to call their own. When Jacob's oldest son, Reuben, found *duadim* ("love plants," which may have been mandrake roots or opium poppies or something else entirely) in the field and gave them to Leah, Rachel traded her apparently prescheduled night with Jacob for the fertility-enhancing flora. The trade seems to have resulted in Leah having three more children and Rachel finally bearing her first: Joseph. Rachel would have only one more biological child, Benjamin, but his birth resulted in her death.

## *Seeing Leah*

She was the biological mother of six tribes and the adoptive mother of two, so why do we know so little about Leah—and why couldn't Jacob love her? Scripture gives us little information about this matriarch to answer those questions.

To start, the meaning of her name is uncertain. It may come from a root that means "weary," or it may mean "wild cow" (in contrast to Rachel's name, which means "ewe"). We know she was the elder sister, and all we are told about her appearance is that her eyes were "weak," which once again is an uncertain translation, and this somehow contrasts Rachel's beauty. She was also perpetually sad, having everything a woman could need by ancient standards (a wealthy husband and many sons of her own) but feeling envious of a long-infertile younger sister who nevertheless had the love of their husband.

I wonder if Leah and Rachel are the intentional female reflection of Esau and Jacob. In both stories we read about the elevation of the younger sibling over the elder. As men, Esau and Jacob could go about their own lives, building their own futures and fortunes as far apart as they wished; but as women, Leah and Rachel were stuck with a lifetime of sibling rivalry because their father married them to the same man. Four hundred or so years later this would be outlawed (Lev. 18:18).

On paper, Leah was the superior sister. She was the oldest, she was obedient to her father, and she was fertile. We don't know what she looked like, but "weak" eyes could mean that she had poor vision or an ophthalmological condition, lacked a vivacious "glint" in her eye, or was constantly crying. But it could also mean that she was a compassionate and dutiful person. She certainly followed her father's instructions to fool Jacob on his first wedding night, and she seems to have accepted Jacob's religion while her sister clung to her household idols (Gen. 31:19).

In the end, Leah got her man if not his love. She was buried in the Cave of Machpelah with Jacob, while Rachel was buried alone on the road to Bethlehem long before the family's interactions with the Egyptians and the fulfillment of Joseph's dreams.

---

The story of seventeen-year-old Joseph receiving his coat, annoying his older brothers with dreams of his own greatness, and being sold as a slave narratively follows a time of change and loss for his elders: God's renaming of Jacob to Israel, Rachel's death after Benjamin's birth, and Isaac's death and burial at Hebron (Gen. 35:10–29). The facts are written directly, with no mention of joy or sorrow, but Jacob does mark the places of his renaming at Bethel and of Rachel's burial on the road to Bethlehem with standing stones. Isaac's tomb needed no such marker as he went into the Cave of Machpelah with his own parents. We may imagine that Jacob and Joseph grieved the loss of Rachel more deeply than Jacob's other children did, and shared grief can certainly knit people together in a unique way. It can also cause irrational behaviors.

Once Jacob and his household had settled down in Canaan, Joseph's story really begins. We read that he was a shepherd who tattled on his half brothers, enjoyed special gifts from Jacob, and boasted about his God-given dreams that implied the brothers would bow down to him. His smart mouth (as my mother would have called it) caused his brothers to intensely hate him and his father to rebuke him (Gen. 37).

I suppose Jacob's reprimand of Joseph was not enough of a punishment for the brothers, as they first concocted a plan to murder him but then decided to sell him instead. It is unclear exactly who bought Joseph, as both Ishmaelites and Midianites are mentioned, but one group of these distant cousins sold him to a government official in Egypt. Maybe it was the last straw—what Jacob thought was the death of his most-loved son on top of the move from Aram to Canaan and the deaths of his favorite wife and aged father—but Jacob grieved this last loss almost to the point of his own death in spite of the comfort offered by his large family and the knowledge that he and his children were favored by God (37:34–35).

## Joseph's Adventures in Egypt

Genesis 39–50 describes Joseph's life in Egypt. Once he arrived, he was sold as a slave to a high-ranking Egyptian official named Potiphar. God was "with Joseph" (37:2), and for that reason everything he did was successful, making his master successful. This was great until Potiphar's wife falsely accused Joseph of rape and he was put in jail. But God remained with Joseph even during his incarceration, and again, everything he did was successful.

Joseph was basically running the jail when the pharaoh imprisoned his cupbearer and baker, both of whom then had disturbing dreams. After Joseph interpreted the men's dreams, the cupbearer went back to work for the pharaoh and two years passed. When Joseph was thirty years old, after thirteen years of slavery and imprisonment, the pharaoh had a dream. The cupbearer remembered Joseph, who was brought in to interpret the dream: Egypt would have seven years of agricultural abundance followed by seven years of famine.

The pharaoh hired Joseph to manage the storage and rationing of Egypt's crops, set him "over all the land of Egypt" as his second in command, and made him a naturalized Egyptian—with an Egyptian name, an Egyptian wife from a priestly family, a royal investiture, and royal symbols such as a signet ring and fine clothes (41:38–45). Joseph went right to work, taking 20 percent of the Egyptians' crops for seven years and then selling the food back to the Egyptians themselves and to foreign refugees for the next seven years. Among those refugees were Joseph's family from Canaan.

So when did Joseph and his family reach Egypt? To place Joseph (or Abram or Moses or anyone else) in the Egyptian timeline, there needs to be a point of agreement between the biblical accounts and the Egyptian records, and we don't have that until 1 Kings 11:40, when Shishak (who many scholars say was Egypt's Shoshenq I) invaded Jerusalem and the temple circa 930 BCE. From that point forward, the Bible often has points of agreement with the historical records of other empires, including Egypt, Neo-Assyria, Neo-Babylonia, Persia, and Rome. From that point backward, we can only consider other types of evidence of cultural interactions, such as shared stories, changing styles, and occasionally loan words.

*Egyptology* is the study of Egypt's culture from about 5000 BCE to around 400 CE. Scholars excavate material remains and read ancient texts that are inscribed on walls, standing stones, and papyrus scrolls. The first two thousand years are *prehistory*, which simply means that writing had not yet been invented. During this time, native people were living in tribes, as Abraham's descendants would two thousand years later in Canaan and Mesopotamia. In 3400 BCE, regional kings started popping up, and in 3100 BCE, a southern king named Narmer united the regions into a nation and founded a capital at Memphis. The first named dynastic phase of the ancient Egyptian timeline is the Old Kingdom, which ran from 2686 to 2121 BCE. This is when the first pyramid—the Step

Pyramid—was built at Saqqara. Later Old Kingdom pharaohs built the pyramids at Giza, including the Great Pyramid, and these structures gave us the first Pyramid Texts. Next came the First Intermediate Period, followed by the Middle Kingdom.[3]

The pharaohs first came into contact with Canaan and Mesopotamia during the Egyptian Middle Kingdom (1991–1786 BCE). This was a time of national expansion for ancient Egypt, and it might be the earliest possible time of interaction between Egypt and the patriarchs. We can't get more exact than that based on the historical records because not every year is accounted for in either the Egyptian historical record or the biblical text. The Egyptian record was often politicized, meaning the reigns of so-called bad pharaohs may have been shortened and the deeds of good pharaohs embellished. As with all of the world's government records, politics influenced exactly what details were recorded and how they were to be remembered by readers.

So instead of counting backward from 930 BCE, the better way to look for overlap between the Egyptians and the Israelites is to consider their cultural shifts. Scholars like to situate Joseph in one of two eras: (1) during the reign of the Hyksos in Egypt's Second Intermediate Period—based on migration patterns; and (2) around the reign of Akhenaten in the New Kingdom—based on a switch to monotheism.

### Who Were the Hyksos?

Imagine what might have been the Egyptians' perspective of this biblical narrative: Joseph was the first foreign *vizier* or "vice pharaoh" in control of Egypt. He allowed for the mass migration of people from Canaan (and likely other regions) to the land of Goshen (Gen. 45:10). These people spoke a different language, were still nomadic, were not experienced in construction, writing, or art, and worshiped a different God. The foreign vizier's policies may have been seen as oppressive by the native Egyptians, especially as he resold only some of the Egyptians' own crops back to them so there would be sustenance for their new foreign neighbors whose population was growing.

So when in Egyptian history did something like that happen? The first time ancient Egypt experienced a cultural (and possibly military) invasion was by the so-called Hyksos people between 1674 and 1567 BCE. We know the Hyksos existed and ruled, but we don't know for sure where they came from or who they were.

The word *Hyksos* is a corruption of an Egyptian phrase meaning "rulers of foreign lands"; it specifically meant rulers of nomadic tribes and was derogatory. Shepherds and nomads were considered dirty and uncultured. The third-century-BCE historian Manetho, who wrote a survey of ancient Egyptian history in Greek and divided it into thirty dynasties, described this outside group growing and taking control of the northern part of an internally fractured Egypt without any violence—but then ruling with iron fists. They set up their government in a northern city called Avaris—which was already populated by immigrants[4]—and ruled for about one century.

Archaeology shows that Avaris was built and settled by people from the Aegean and the Levant. The excavations of Manfred Bietak focused on the Canaanite material culture throughout the site, including Canaanite-style architecture, ceramics, and burials.[5] Canaanites definitely settled there, but they weren't entirely alone, as Egypt was surrounded by several nomadic groups. There is evidence of cultural blending; the Hyksos kept their architectural styles and their names, but they took on some aspects of Egyptian culture, including government practices, writing styles, and worship of the Egyptian god Seth.

The Hyksos left no mention of a man named Joseph as the vizier of Egypt, they were in Egypt one hundred years instead of four hundred years, and their downfall was one of conquest, not exodus as the Bible describes for the Israelites. All in all, this theory for the peaceful arrival and rise of the Israelites as Hyksos in Egypt is compelling but not perfect. What it does show is a solid connection between the populations of Egypt and the Levant during the time the patriarchs probably lived. But another possibility for Joseph's rise in Egypt occurred two hundred years later.

### Who Was Akhenaten?

The expulsion of the Hyksos ushered in the New Kingdom era (1567–1085 BCE) of Egyptian history. During that period, Egypt began thinking like an empire. The pharaohs weren't just trading with surrounding nations; they were attacking and conquering, or at least subjugating, them. They were taking the wealth of the empire and building temples and cities and tombs. The New Kingdom was, in many ways, the zenith of ancient Egyptian culture; it was the time with pharaohs whose names you know: Hatshepsut, Tutankhamun, and Rameses (all eleven of them!).

Ruling in the middle of those more famous names was a man named Amenhotep IV, who renamed himself Akhenaten. He only reigned for seventeen years, from 1379 to 1362 BCE, but he made drastic structural changes to life in Egypt.

Ancient Egyptian religion was incredibly complex, and it changed over time. It was, of course, polytheistic. Across ancient cultures, humans who lacked scientific explanations for the natural world developed rituals and gods they could bribe for better lives; therefore, most of the gods were tied to nature, as we see in ancient Greek traditions: Zeus threw thunderbolts, Demeter promoted crop growth, Hades collected the dead underground, and so on. Worship was intended to keep the world spinning, and in Egypt, that meant keeping the Nile flooding and the sun rising.

During the New Kingdom, Egypt's head god was Amun-Ra. He was considered the creator god, who made all that we see and all of the other gods. Everyone was worshiping him, and pharaohs took his name: Amenhotep means something like "Amun is satisfied" or "Amun is at peace."

When Amenhotep IV came to power, Egyptians believed the sun's disk was the god Aten—important for renewal and rebirth but not the top god. Surmising that Aten is light and light is life, Amenhotep IV elevated him first to the highest god and then to the only god. He moved the administration of Egypt from Thebes to Amarna (which is why this is called the Amarna Period). He built a brand-new city, changed his name to Akhenaten ("helpful to Aten"), and created a new essentially monotheistic religion. Unlike Amun and others in the Egyptian pantheon, Aten was a silent god; the pharaoh spoke for him.

No sacred texts have been found, so we don't know much about the short-lived religion. It seems that "worship" meant Egyptian citizens abandoning Amun and being totally loyal to the pharaoh. Any lingering loyalties to Amun were treated as a state crime. Akhenaten tried to have all mentions of Amun erased; writings and sculptures were desecrated. Because of the way the god was "persecuted," Amun—which means "the Hidden One"—continued to be heralded by the weak and poor in Egyptian society.

Because of the disproportionate amount of time Akhenaten spent propagating his new religion, many of the political and civic responsibilities would necessarily have fallen to his vizier. It was important for the pharaoh to trust his vizier because he was the only person with enough power to potentially overthrow the monarchy. For this reason, Akhenaten would have been more likely to trust a monotheist who shared his values concerning religion. And that seems to have happened—in a man named 'Abdiel who rose to power under Amenhotep III and served throughout his and Akhenaten's reigns.

'Abdiel means "servant of the god El." His name honored El, as the pharaohs' names honored their gods Amun or Aten. El was a god in many of the Semitic tribes, and we even see that name in one of the Israelites' titles for God, Elohim, and in the names of His followers, such as Samuel and Daniel.

Everything we know about 'Abdiel comes from his tomb at Saqqara. Even though the tomb had been plundered, his wealth and status were obvious. He, his wife, and one son were each buried in not two but three nested coffins. Grave goods included canopic jars, impressive gold and beaded jewelry, and inscriptions. He was called "vizier," "child of the palace," and "father of the god [meaning the pharaoh]." Those titles reveal his closeness to both Amenhotep III and Akhenaten as administrator, childhood friend, and parental figure. He was, in every way we can see, a cultural Egyptian who happened to have a Semitic name and possibly a Semitic heritage.[6]

Just as the entrance of the Hyksos to Egypt didn't perfectly fit the Genesis narrative, neither do the details of 'Abdiel's life, death, and burial match Joseph's. Joseph was embalmed and entombed in Egypt, but at his request, Moses later took his body and returned it to the land of Canaan (Exod. 13:19). All we can say from the discovery of 'Abdiel is that the ascension of someone with non-Egyptian heritage to the second-highest position in government happened during a time of political upheaval. Although Joseph's story cannot be dated, Egyptian artifacts and records show it to be plausible and help us to envision what his life may have looked like in Egypt.

## Joseph's Relation to the Twelve Tribes

In the genealogies, Joseph is not listed among the patriarchs of Israel: Abraham, Isaac, and Jacob. He is not the head of one of the twelve tribes, even though he was one of the twelve sons of Jacob and one of the two sons of Rachel. Joseph's descendants apparently needed a different path to becoming Israelites, which may have been the result of Joseph's stronger cultural attachment to Egypt than to Canaan in his adulthood. The pharaoh had renamed Joseph as Zaphnath-Paaneah, made him de facto ruler of the nation, and given him an Egyptian wife whose father was a priest. He was culturally Egyptian.

At Jacob's deathbed, he gave his name to Joseph's two oldest sons, Manasseh and Ephraim, making them into "sons of Israel" instead of "sons of Joseph" (Gen. 48:1–12). Their descendants would later be known as the two "half-tribes" of Joseph and would occasionally be called the "house of Joseph" when they were working together. Eventually the symbolic meaning of the "house of Joseph" grew to mean all ten tribes of Israel's Northern Kingdom, as the half-tribe of Ephraim became the most politically powerful of the ten once his descendant Jeroboam took the throne.

Although it may not have been clear to Jacob at the time, there is a second reason he needed two more descendants. In Joshua 13, after the Israelites have taken Canaan and as land is being allotted to the tribes, the tribe of Levi does not receive property because "the LORD God of Israel was their inheritance" (v. 33). Once Israel became a nation, the Levites lived in and around the other tribes' territories. Their life's work would be serving God, not cultivating land or building cities, so they would be materially supported by the other tribes. Jacob needed both Ephraim and Manasseh to "replace" Joseph and Levi.

## Conclusion

The story of Joseph's life is the longest narrative in Genesis, filling the last quarter of the book. He is a precocious dreamer, a hard worker, a patient prisoner, a dedicated servant, a talented prankster, and a loving family man. His story captivates readers and storytellers alike because it has sorrow and joy, struggle and triumph, hatred and love. Still, Joseph is an unexpected theological bridge between the patriarchs and Moses, as he doesn't really factor in the future of the Israelites because his own sons took their grandfather's name and abandoned his. However, Joseph's adventures in Egypt are the very beginning of the exodus story that will bring about the development of his family's worship of God into the entire Israelite religion.

Joseph teaches us that the key to thriving in another culture, no matter how we got there, is faith in God. He doesn't stubbornly cling to the traditions he grew up with or run back to Canaan as soon as he has the chance. Instead, he lives a life of devotion throughout his unexpected and often unwanted circumstances that God uses to bless everyone around him. His choice to serve God in the worst and best of times, whether he is alone among strangers or surrounded by family, is an example for all who read Genesis and specifically for people who find themselves displaced from their homelands and loved ones by circumstances. This has been practically true for the Jewish people since 586 BCE, and it is metaphorically true for all Christians who are citizens of heaven (Eph. 2:19).

God is always with His children no matter where they are, and as the Israelites looked forward to the arrival of their Messiah, we Christians look back at and give thanks for Emmanuel, God with us. Joseph teaches us that, in the words of Sir Tim Rice, "children of Israel are never alone," be they in a pit, in a prison, or in a palace. In exile or at home.

# Moses's Big Exit

Webber and Rice may have presented Joseph's coat as Technicolor, but Cecil B. DeMille famously filmed the entire exodus that way! Released on November 8, 1956, *The Ten Commandments* made history as the most expensive film ever made at that time, and it was also DeMille's most financially successful project, his first widescreen production, and the last film he ever directed.[1]

One key to the movie's continuing popularity throughout the last seventy years is its entrance into our homes. *The Ten Commandments* has been appointment viewing every Holy Week. I look forward to it more than *Rudolph the Red-Nosed Reindeer* during the Christmas season! With a complete running time of three hours thirty-nine minutes—when both DeMille's introduction and the intermission are included—broadcast versions of the film run well over four hours with the addition of commercials. In the United States, ABC began airing it in 1973 and still does so each year, although it is starting to move to digital platforms since the length has always been problematic for television station schedules and viewers now expect almost all entertainment on demand.

The film is epic not only in its length but also in its cultural reach. Its brilliant colorful images have so pervaded our lives that when we read the Exodus account, we picture Moses as Charlton Heston and the unnamed pharaoh as Yul Brynner's Rameses II. We envision the Red Sea splitting open instantly, creating walls of water that resemble aquarium exhibits. We might unconsciously insert characters who aren't in the text, such as Queen Nefretiri, and imagine episodes between her and Moses that didn't happen in Scripture but are so memorable.

To fill the screen and the time for his epic production, DeMille claimed to have taken the extra characters and extra scenes from historical sources, such as Jewish midrash and the writings of Josephus. However, he made no distinctions between his presentations of biblical and historical sources and fiction. DeMille narrates the film with the same rich voice and authority when he is reading passages from Exodus, Numbers, and Deuteronomy as when he is reading the script. This makes for an engaging viewing experience but leaves many Bible readers conflating DeMille's art and God's Scripture.

Much of the biblical narrative concerning the Israelites' flight from Egypt and move toward Canaan is included in the book of Exodus, but the texts that follow—Leviticus, Numbers, and Deuteronomy— are the practical outgrowths of Moses's story. Those four books, plus Genesis 1:28 and 32:32, include the laws that would dictate the Israelites' social interactions and worship practices. They may seem like boring reads when they are recounting which animals were to be sacrificed or how society should deal with criminals in their midst, but they became the foundation for ancient Israelite life and continue to shape modern Jewish communities. The 613 laws, as they have been counted since the third century CE, may not be as "spectacular" as the depiction of Moses's life in *The Ten Commandments*, but they are a Bible reader's first practical connection to an awesome God.

## Who Wrote the Torah?

The first five books of the Bible are their own special collection that has several names: the Torah, which means "law"; the Pentateuch, which means "five volumes"; and the Five Books of Moses. However, the idea that Moses wrote Genesis, Exodus, Leviticus, Numbers, and Deuteronomy in their entirety is not a scriptural one. The books' authorship was debated by Jewish scholars for many centuries, and crediting Moses as the writer from Genesis 1:1 through his death in Deuteronomy 34:5 (at which point they state authorship was assumed by Joshua) was codified as Jewish tradition by the Babylonian Talmud around 500 CE.[2]

### *Sourcing Tradition*

Ask a Christian what is Scripture, and that person will pull out a Bible. All of the holy books are bound together in one place. All divine authority is between those covers. We may supplement our studies with the writings of humans, but no one should be holding up the words of Lewis, Calvin, Luther, or even the saints as equal to the Word of God.

In the Jewish tradition, the Hebrew Bible (the Old Testament, just in a different order with different verse numbers) is also the only Scripture. But for thousands of years, rabbis have engaged in rhetorical exercises with the Bible and each other. Their oral conversations, arguments, and conclusions were compiled into the written Babylonian Talmud, Jerusalem Talmud, and many volumes of midrash (which is a literal "inquiry" into Scripture's nature and applications) between the second and fourteenth centuries CE. Those sources may not be divine, but they have great authority over Jewish beliefs, traditions, and practices, and many of them influenced Christian traditions as well.

Those of us who grew up with the tradition of Mosaic authorship of the Torah may have been told that he sat down and wrote the first version of world and Israelite history in Hebrew on an ancient leather scroll while wandering between Egypt and the promised land. But his involvement in the recording of ancient history was more likely as a speaker of oral traditions that would eventually be recorded once better tools were invented, written language was more fully developed, and literacy had expanded.

Based on its form, vocabulary, and grammar, the Song of the Sea (Exod. 15:1–18, which is often titled the "Song of Moses" by the publishers of Christian Bibles) is one of the oldest passages in the Bible. It is lyric poetry, which is not surprising, considering the likely low rate of literacy among the ancient Israelites. Moses might have composed this first history lesson for his followers as a song because the format would make memorizing the events of the Red Sea crossing easier, and he wanted the Israelites to be able to accurately teach future generations how God protected His people on their way out of Egypt.

About one-third of the Hebrew Bible is written in poetry. You find it sprinkled throughout the narrative books (such as Gen. 1 and Judg. 5), but it dominates Psalms, Proverbs, Job, and many of the Prophets. The poetry of the Hebrew Bible, when translated into English and other modern languages, does not typically retain the literary structure, artistic language, and musical rhythm that would have been obvious to original audiences and aided in memorization.

In the ancient world as today, it is easier to memorize a passage that rhymes or is set to a tune. As a child I loved the "Fruits of the Spirit" song with coconuts and watermelons and silly faces; as an adult I appreciate the fact that it taught me Galatians 5:22–23: "But the fruit of the Spirit is love, joy, peace, longsuffering, kindness, goodness, faithfulness, gentleness, self-control." I doubt the apostle Paul anticipated his letter becoming a VBS standard á la "Father Abraham," but simple words set to a simple tune helped me learn about God and His Word long before I could read those words for myself. Oral tradition had and has great value.

### From Moses's Oral Traditions to the Jews' Handwritten Texts

For hundreds of years, scholars have debated when exactly the first Scriptures were recorded.

Considering all discovered media—from walls and pottery with ancient graffiti to jewelry and scrolls with careful inscriptions—arguably the oldest biblical text archaeologists have found is pressed into a tiny silver scroll from Ketef Hinnom that someone would have worn as a remembrance on a necklace in the sixth century BCE.[3] It contains a simple version of Numbers 6:24–26, which states, "The LORD bless you and keep you; the LORD make His face shine upon you, and be gracious to you; the LORD lift up His countenance upon you, and give you peace." In a largely illiterate ancient society, someone took the time to write a scriptural blessing on a costly piece of silver that the owner assumed would never again be read once finished.

Until scribes began diligently recording the Hebrew Scriptures onto leather and papyrus scrolls for use in the temple and later in synagogues and churches around the world, God's words were known through long-told stories and memorized prayers passed down within families from generation to generation. Why did it take so long for written Scripture to proliferate? Because texts required skill, time, and resources to create.

Consider the scribes mentioned in the Hebrew Bible: Each one served in a wealthy king's administration, be it for Israel or a foreign power. David's and Solomon's often nameless scribes pop up all over Samuel and Kings. Ezra, who famously led the rebuilding of Jerusalem's temple after the exile, did so at the command of the Persian king Artaxerxes, whom he served as the court's Jewish attaché (Ezra 7:6). Even Baruch, who served as the prophet Jeremiah's personal scribe, came from a noble family of royal scribes.[4]

Government involvement in scribal work continued during the Hellenistic period (332–330 BCE, which we will discuss in chapter 10), after Alexander the Great had conquered the ancient Near

East. As his Greek traditions were imposed across his newly won empire, nationalism arose among the Jews and the dissemination of Scripture became important no matter who was king. Scribes began copying scrolls in earnest, and around 250 BCE, Ptolemy II of Egypt even requested a Greek translation of the Hebrew Scriptures for his library at Alexandria. The men who had learned how to write the Hebrew alphabet began copying the as-yet uncanonized biblical books letter by letter onto scrolls. If they made a mistake—no matter how close they were to completing the scroll—it would be buried and never read.

Although we have evidence of Scripture fragments being written in the sixth century BCE if not earlier, the first complete version of the Hebrew Bible—called the Leningrad Codex—was made in 1008 CE, and the oldest copy of Ptolemy II's Greek translation—called the Codex Sinaiticus and including the New Testament—was made around 350 CE. Having all biblical writings combined into one scroll or one book is relatively new. And having access to those books whenever we want, whether in a hotel nightstand or on a smartphone app, is a luxury we take for granted today.

### What Is Source Criticism?

So if Moses didn't sit down and write every word of the Torah as he was leading the Israelites through the wilderness, then where did those Scriptures come from? This question has been widely debated for millennia, but consensus began to form in 1885. A German biblical scholar named Julius Wellhausen wrote a series of articles describing four sources who recorded the oral traditions that would become the Torah. He named the sources the Yahwist (J—because in German, a *j* sounds like an English *y*), the Elohist (E), the Priestly source (P), and the Deuteronomist (D). Each source was unique in its style, theme, vocabulary, and even chronology, and all had been put together by later redactors to give us the Bible we have today.[5]

Wellhausen's Documentary Hypothesis, as this theory is widely known, has evolved over time because, as I like to say, nothing is settled so long as exploration continues. As archaeologists continue to unearth documents and as scholars better understand the development of ancient languages, the exact sources and the ways those writers interacted with each other's work must be reexamined. Maybe the Torah and the rest of the Hebrew Bible are not simply a combination of the exact four independent sources identified by Wellhausen, but the books do show signs of multiple sources building upon each other's writings to create what we read today.[6]

All we can really know for certain is what the Bible itself tells us: The Torah and most subsequent books were written anonymously and are inspired by God. The exact dates and form of development should be less important to the reader than the theological content—although the history is awfully fun to investigate and I consider any interaction with Scripture to be worthwhile!

### Thank You, Professor Schwartz

After finishing a class in the spring of 2004, Dr. Baruch J. Schwartz motioned to a few of his graduate students as we were leaving the lecture hall. He had been planning a workshop for the following Thursday night and invited six of us to attend. He gave us no details about what we would be doing, but when I hesitated because of household commitments, he said, "Bring your husband!" For so many reasons, I am glad David was invited. He may have loved the evening even more than I did, and he definitely recounts this story better than I can.

Dr. Schwartz was a visiting professor from Hebrew University that semester. I was taking his course titled "Israel's Prophets as Messengers of God," but we would soon learn that he had a tangential interest in the origins of Scripture.[7]

Ten of us arrived at a section room in Andover Hall about seven o'clock that evening. It was a small interior room with no windows

81

and no air conditioning, dark wainscoting that crept three-quarters of the way up the wall, and a giant solid wood table that left barely enough room for chairs. Dr. Schwartz was already in there distributing papers with Scripture fragments from Exodus printed all over them. At the top of each page was a letter: J, E, or P. "You've all learned about the Documentary Hypothesis, haven't you? Tonight you are going to redact the Bible the way we think the first scribes did." Dr. Schwartz had us begin by reading Exodus 19 aloud. "Stop whenever something sounds like it is being repeated," he told us.

> In the third month after the children of Israel had gone out of the land of Egypt, on the same day, they *came to the Wilderness of Sinai*. For they had departed from Rephidim, *had come to the Wilderness of Sinai*, and *camped in the wilderness*. So Israel *camped there before the mountain*. (vv. 1–2)

We marked our Bibles, and then continued the exercise for the rest of the chapter. We realized that over the three days described in Exodus 19, Moses went up and down Mount Sinai four times. Today, experienced hikers on well-worn paths of Egypt's Jabal Mousa (the peak traditionally associated with Mount Sinai) can go from the base to St. Catherine's Monastery at the 7,497-foot summit in about three hours (so that's six hours round trip). Assuming that we've identified the right mountain, that Moses's lungs and muscles were robust, and that God blazed a path for him in the untamed wilderness, Moses was actively hiking at least twenty-four out of ninety-six hours to an elevation well above that of Denver, Colorado. That's impressive and impractical.

Dr. Schwartz then guided us to evaluate our work. "Take a look at the papers in front of you. Each one represents what I believe the complete texts of the J, E, and P sources looked like before redactors put them together. If you were editing the final version of the Torah—and you believed that all sources are divinely inspired—how would you put them together?"

We all agreed: "Wherever the sources say the same thing, write it down once. Wherever the sources disagree, include both versions. Delete nothing." We did just that with the J, E, and P sources, and we ended up writing exactly what is in Exodus 19.

At the end of the evening, Dr. Schwartz explained why he had done this exercise. I remember him saying he was a theologian who believes in the Bible while working for secular institutions. Most Bible scholars who accept the Documentary Hypothesis use it to prove that the Bible is not divinely inspired but is the work of people. He saw the opposite, that four different versions of the Torah existed, and when the scribes sat down to combine them, they made no choices and no changes to any of them because all four were divinely inspired—as were the scribes themselves.

Prior to this evening, I had considered my relationship with Scripture a bit fractured: I had a deep faith in God, but I had spent the previous four years having every Christian tradition I'd grown up with be challenged by scholars. When presented with the fact that Moses died prior to the end of Deuteronomy and could not possibly have written the account of his own burial, I learned the information but walled it off, unable to reconcile my belief in the Bible's inerrancy with the work of philologists. The presence of doublets, the variances between Kings and Chronicles, and the late vocabularies used in early stories such as Job had always been presented to me as errors. But Dr. Schwartz's perspective—that the God-following scribes intentionally included all of the so-called errors because they believed every part was divinely inspired—put me back together.

As someone who has now spent many years editing hundreds of theological manuscripts and writing several books of my own, I would add to his reasoning that no editor or author worth his or her salt would allow such "errors" to remain. I would guide an author to choose if Noah's animals boarded two by two or seven by two, or to add more details to Abram and Sarai's exploits with the two kings so they weren't so similar. But the scribes did not do that, because they knew the words before them were given by God. They didn't need to be edited, only written down for posterity. This shift in perspective—from seeing errors as evidence of human intervention to evidence of divine origination—allows us to question those difficult passages without abandoning our faith.

## Sinai's Golden Calf

The most iconic image from *The Ten Commandments* is the gold, life-sized adolescent cow that DeMille based on Exodus 32 and the Egyptian goddess Hathor. The director must have read the chapter and thought the Israelites could only have been imitating the culture they had just fled, so he crafted a scene of polite debauchery illustrating his imagining of Egyptian-style worship of the goddess of beauty, music, dancing, and fertility.

But maybe he got it all wrong. To start, just a bunch of earrings (v. 2) would never make something the size DeMille imagined! More importantly, consider how the Israelites responded to the calf: "This is your god, O Israel, that brought you out of the land of Egypt!" (v. 4). Having been saved from the plagues, experienced the Passover, and followed God as a column of cloud and fire, how likely is it that the people chose to credit an Egyptian fertility goddess with saving them?

I think something else is happening here. The Israelites were scared. At the time Aaron molded the calf, Moses had been up on the mountain so long that everyone thought he was dead (v. 1). Obviously they'd lost faith in God's and Moses's promises to them, so they tried to take matters into their own hands. Not knowing exactly how to worship their own God, they likely leaned on the practices of the cultures around them. Yes, Egypt had gods shaped like cows, but the Canaanites, who lived in the land their ancestors had left and to which they were returning, worshiped gods who sat on cows. El rode a bull, while his son, Ba'al, rode a calf. In Canaanite Ashkelon, a "golden calf" was found in his own clay shrine inside a 1600 BCE sanctuary just right of the city gate. He could stand easily on an adult's open hand, and his bronze (no, not literally gold) body was once overlaid with silver. His clay house was much taller than him, leaving room for an invisible rider.[8]

The Israelites' God was unseen, and if He had a mount, they didn't know about it yet. So maybe Aaron intended to cast a throne for their unseen God that would call Him back to them. The text seems to support this interpretation because the feast day they were honoring was God's (v. 5), not Hathor's or a calf's. We modern readers certainly know better than to make a molded image of God, but might we try to entice Him down to us when we feel abandoned? Absolutely.

Notice how quickly God followed the golden calf episode with the making of His ark. He renews His covenant with the Israelites and then sets about giving them something physical to represent His presence and contain the stone tablets of testimony. God instructs the Israelites to build a tent for Him where He can meet with Moses closer to the camps, and then to craft the ark with its cherubim-topped cover (Exod. 34–37). Wherever the ark would rest—in that tent or later in the temple—God would "sit" above the cherubim's wings. And the people had a place to worship in His presence.

---

### "Evidence" of the Exodus?

Just as the Egyptian records had no direct evidence of Joseph, they also have no mention of Moses, the plagues, or the Israelites' dramatic escape. In the absence of an obvious Egyptian accounting of the exodus, we must look at Scripture and ancient Egyptian history and consider theories that aren't in Technicolor!

If you google "When was the exodus?" you will get dates ranging from 1600 BCE to 1300 BCE. I've even heard one passionately wrong person insist it happened in the 900s. There is as little consensus about the dates of Moses's years on earth as there is about Joseph's, but we do get a classical date of the early 1200s—during the reign of Rameses II—for a not-so-good reason. The name Rameses is in the Bible four times (Gen. 47:11; Exod. 12:37; Num. 33:3, 5), and in each instance, the name refers to a place, not a person. But that hasn't stopped generations of people associating a city's name with the most famous pharaoh of Egyptian history. Sunday school teachers taught me that the pharaoh of the exodus was Rameses the Great, and Cecil B. DeMille reinforced that with *The Ten Commandments*.

In the Bible, the pharaoh is unnamed; in the Egyptian record, the exodus is not recorded. Instead of accepting that a lack of supporting evidence indicates the exodus was not a historical event, or embracing Hollywood fiction as fact, scholars and armchair intellectuals alike have theories about when and how the events of Exodus 7–12 unfolded. Let's take a look at the most popular one.

### The Santorini Theory

In 2006, James Cameron (who directed *Jaws*, *Terminator*, *Titanic*, *Avatar*, and other blockbuster films) and Simcha Jacobovici (who adopted the moniker of Naked Archaeologist, although he is neither naked nor an archaeologist) produced a movie called *The Exodus Decoded*.[9] In it, the men claimed to have a new explanation for the exodus event, but all they really did was reintroduce and illustrate an old theory with trips to archaeological sites and impressive-for-the-time graphics.

In 1981, Dr. Hans Goedicke, an Egyptologist at Johns Hopkins University, first argued the exodus occurred in 1477 BCE. He based this on his translation of a royal Egyptian inscription from the reign of female pharaoh Hatshepsut and the geological evidence that the eruption of Santorini's volcano around 1475 BCE flooded the Nile Delta.[10] He and subsequent scholars have argued that the eruption triggered many natural disasters that could have caused the miraculous plagues of Exodus 7–11, although in a different order than the Bible describes. The theory makes the following assertions:

1. The volcano erupted seven cubic miles of magma and sent a plume of ash twenty-seven miles into the air, darkening the skies as described in the ninth plague (10:21–22).

2. Thunder and hail and fire from the sky corresponded to the seventh plague (9:23–25), and the humidity following the storms would have been favorable for the locusts of the eighth plague (10:12–14).

3. Subsequent earthquakes released iron oxide that turned the water red with rust (like the blood of the first plague in 7:19–21). The iron oxide then made the waters uninhabitable for the fish (7:18) and frogs (second plague, 8:6–13) and undrinkable for the livestock, who then died (fifth plague, 9:6) and attracted swarms of flies (fourth plague, 8:24).

4. The earthquakes also released carbon monoxide that would have killed anyone sleeping on a bed instead of on the floor, which in Egyptian society was an honor reserved for first-born sons. The gas would have suffocated the boys and men as they slept, as described in the tenth plague (12:29–30).

5. The earthquakes finally caused a tsunami that pulled back the waters of the Mediterranean, allowing the Israelites to cross on dry land before the wave crashed over the pursuing Egyptian army and refilled the delta as described in Exodus 14.

At first glance, the theory is compelling. In what the Bible describes as a series of miracles, scholars argue that historically proven natural disasters were misinterpreted by Exodus as acts of God. But as so often happens with broad theories, the points that do not fit were conveniently left out or explained away by supporters. Twenty-five years later, the movie *Decoding the Exodus* added to the theory, making many more errors in the process:

1. The film tries to argue that Amosis was the pharaoh of the exodus based on the fragmented Tempest Stele they say describes the exodus events, even though they admit to having never seen it. The stele, which is a large upright

stone engraved with words and possibly lost images com-
memorating important events, probably does describe the
strange weather associated with the eruption on Santorini,
but that's it.

2. They "synchronize" the date of the exodus to 1500 with
   clips from scholars. Sometimes they pick the argument
   they like best; other times they divide the differences between the numbers. Neither method is sound scholarship.

3. The artifacts the film highlights are not fully described.
   For example, evidence for the parting of the water is credited to another stele written in the 300s by a Ptolemaic
   pharaoh about a different god. It's from the wrong time,
   by the wrong writer, and about the wrong story; but because it mentions water "dividing," the film then adjusts
   the Santorini theory to state the Israelites crossed the El
   Balah Lake.

4. The film implies that the Egyptian government is trying
   to hide any finds related to Israel by having antiquities au-
   thorities cover the dig sites annually. As all archaeologists
   know, seasons end by excavators re-covering exposed soil
   layers and artifacts with sandbags and dirt to protect what
   is coming out of the ground from robbers, animals, and
   the elements, and to protect lost humans from falling into
   giant pits.

Whenever you watch documentaries, remember that they are
not pure history. They are designed to entertain and make a point.
I enjoy the work of Ken Burns, but even his highly acclaimed series
set out to tell stories, not to give you all the raw facts of history.
Textbooks should do that, but they don't make millions for their
authors and are more likely to put us to sleep than to captivate us.

In pieces like *The Exodus Decoded*, it is important to know who
is behind the film and what agendas they may have. What have they

chosen to leave out? What have they misunderstood? What have they fabricated? How have they edited the scholars' words? This film is the ultimate example of proof-texting, as facts are pulled out of their own contexts and strung together to support an idea.

### The Parting of Waters

What was the name of the sea that God separated for the Israelites as they were following Moses out of Egypt? In the prose description of the events, the water is simply called "the sea" (Exod. 14:26–29), but in the older poetry version, the water is identified as "the Red Sea" (15:4). But your Bible translation is deceiving you unless it includes a footnote on verse 4 that reads something like "lit. Sea of Reeds."

In the Hebrew, the words that our Bibles tend to render as "Red Sea" are *yam suph*. *Yam* means "sea," but *suph* is a little trickier. What *suph* does not mean is "red." The word we would translate as "red" is *adom*, as in that guy named Adam whom God created from rich, red-colored dirt and whose skin could be reddened by the sun. Obviously this is a common word that would have been known to Moses as he composed the Song of the Sea, so if he had meant "Red Sea," then I think he would have sung it.

So why have Bible translators knowingly mistranslated *yam suph* for so long? Tradition. The first translation of the Hebrew Bible is the Greek translation called the Septuagint, which was commissioned by Ptolemy II. It made the first attempt to "correct" what presumably had been written in the even older Hebrew manuscripts we no longer have today. It replaced what we would call a common noun and adjective, *yam suph*, with a proper noun, Red Sea, presumably in an attempt to help readers more quickly understand where the actions were taking place.

Other translations then followed the Septuagint's lead without really questioning whether the addition was correct. It is impossible to know exactly why the translators of the Septuagint decided to edit the Hebrew, but the best idea I've heard is that *yam suph* is used in other places in the Bible where other geographical details make it clear that those writers were referring to the Red Sea, as we call it today. For example, "King Solomon also built a fleet of ships at Ezion Geber, which is near Elath on the shore of the *yam suph*, in the land of Edom" (1 Kings 9:26). There is little doubt that this passage is talking about our Red Sea based on the three other locations mentioned. But the problem is, we can't assume that *yam suph* always means the Red Sea.

So if it doesn't mean "red," then what does *suph* mean? Most scholars today will tell you it comes to Hebrew from an Egyptian word that means "reed." *Yam suph* translates to "Reed Sea" and describes a shallow body of water where papyrus reeds can grow. A lot of researchers really like this idea because it makes God's dividing of the sea naturally possible and not necessarily miraculous: A strong wind would be enough to carve a path in a papyrus marsh. Of course, it is then difficult to imagine an entire army drowning in the same papyrus marsh!

So maybe we don't yet understand what the ancient writers meant by *suph*. In 1984, religious studies professor Bernard Batto suggested that *suph* might not be an Egyptian loanword meaning "reed" but may in fact be related to the Hebrew word *soph*, meaning "end."[11] This results in *yam suph* meaning something like "sea at the end [of the world]." In that case, the improper noun *yam suph* could describe any large body of water where a distant shore could not be seen. In the ancient Near East, this could have described the Red Sea, the Mediterranean Sea, or even the Persian Gulf.

The "end" translation never caught on in theological circles, but its sheer reasonableness reminds me that no one knows everything. When it comes to Scripture and history, there are no easy, exact, perfect answers. I happen to think that is part of God's design because it keeps us curious and engaging with the Bible. But my comfort with "I don't know" is unusual in a world that demands certainty. Some people feel the need to prove the Bible, and often that leads to falsehood being accepted as fact. Sometimes it is easier to believe a lie than to challenge the person presenting it or to live with uncertainty.

Every few years, just as you might hear about Noah's ark or the ark of the covenant being discovered (only for the debunking to never make headlines), images of "the pharaoh's chariots" at the bottom of the Red Sea make the rounds on social media. None of those items have been found, and there isn't even consensus about where we should be looking. But the false stories still make headlines and gain clicks because naturally we are all curious to see them! If you've seen the chariot wheels or even so-called horse corpses in photographs, you've probably been shown the remnants of one of more than two dozen shipwrecks, including ships' helms posing as chariot wheels. Those images get doctored and deep-faked, but they still bring in clicks.

When it comes to the exodus, there is no physical evidence (so far). What we have is an explanation of how God miraculously altered His creation to free the Israelites. Nothing in the Exodus account is likely to leave behind archaeological evidence except maybe some army equipment, which—again—has not been found. There's no reason Egypt would have wanted to record the event in its history, as it would have been politically damaging to the pharaoh who lost his army in pursuit of slaves. The current fact that we have no evidence is okay. It's even good! Because typically God's miracles leave behind only awe and wonderment and the faith of the people who witnessed them.

## Conclusion

Why do I spend so much time considering what the ancient world looked like when it seems the investigations never confirm the historicity of biblical events? Because understanding the cultures and customs in and around ancient Israel helps us to understand Scripture better. History cannot replace God's Word, but it is important for helping us bridge the time gaps between the stories being told and the lives we live today. It is better to know historical Egyptian and Canaanite representations of their bull idols than to allow a secular and fantastical filmmaker—great though DeMille was—to interpret a sacred text for us.

As I say all the time, biblical archaeology does not exist to prove the Bible. It contextualizes it. This is especially true for miracles. Miracles, by definition, are acts of God that violate our laws of physics and cannot be proven. While it is entirely possible that God would choose to use natural phenomena such as a volcanic eruption to create a miracle, it is more likely that the plagues, the parting of the Red Sea, and the columns of cloud and fire from heaven were one-time interventions of the Creator God. When we read Exodus, we should be impressed by the power He wields within His creation and His willingness to intervene on grand and small levels for the good of His people.

The miracles of the exodus were particularly awesome in the literal sense of the word. They inspired awe and wonder and fear in Israelites and Egyptians alike because no one doubted they were acts of God and not just weather patterns. In the end, it wasn't the plagues or deaths themselves that convinced the pharaoh to set the Israelites free; it was his recognition of the power and reality of the Israelites' God. He told them to "go, serve the LORD as you have said," but then added, "and bless me also" (Exod. 12:31–32). The king of Egypt—who was believed to be a god by his people and by himself—asked to be blessed by his former slaves in the name of the God they worshiped. That recognition and moment of humility in a megalomaniac is its own kind of miracle!

# David's Duel with a "Giant"

On the Mediterranean coast, thirty-five miles south of Tel Aviv and twelve miles north of the Gaza Strip, sits the modern and ancient city of Ashkelon. In the Iron Age, it was one of the Philistines' five capital cities, and in 2004, it was the first site where I dug alongside other grad students from Harvard and a few other universities. That season we spent a lot of time excavating a home and the street that ran alongside it. The work was hot and heavy, and we all looked forward to when we could climb out of the deep pit excavators had been digging for two decades and eat a second breakfast underneath a wild fig tree. The breezes from the Mediterranean were a comfort, as were the cold eggs and fresh tomatoes and cucumbers that were delivered to us each day.

We had no electricity at our square, and we were a few years ahead of smart devices that would play music to pass the time. Inspired by the marvelous (if eventually monotonous) vegetables we consumed each day, one volunteer cut a mouth into his cucumber and began to sing: "If you like to talk to tomatoes / If a squash can make you smile . . ." Groans abounded from the Americans, but the Israeli students were confused. We told them about Veggie-Tales, the cartoon series dedicated to teaching children the morals behind Bible stories.

Among the original VeggieTales episodes is *Dave and the Giant Pickle*, which narrator Bob the Tomato explains is "a story about a boy named Dave. . . . Of all of the brothers, he was the small-est."[1] Dave is a prepubescent asparagus who is bullied by his larger gourd-brothers and spends his days helping vertigo-plagued sheep stand up in their sandy desert home. One day when his brothers are with King Saul's army facing a Philistine champion named Goliath, Dave arrives with stuffed-crust pizza for the soldiers and decides to face Goliath himself. With a tiny sling, he hits the pickle on the head, knocks him to the ground, and wins the day for Is-rael's army. Bob goes on to explain, "In our story, no one thought David could do anything important. After all, he was just a little guy! . . . But David loved God, and he knew that even though he was small, God could help him do big things."

In their retelling of 1 Samuel 17 for children, VeggieTales leans into the world's popular interpretation of the original David ver-sus Goliath battle. They emphasize how unevenly matched the two participants are, as sports commentators might talk about an unranked team facing a national champion or as political pundits might view a stay-at-home mom running against a longtime in-cumbent. The disparity between the opponents foreshadows one of two outcomes: Either the favorite wins as expected or God performs a miracle so the weakling prevails.

The David versus Goliath confrontation is scriptural, but the "God of the underdogs" meaning we ascribe to it comes from popular depictions of the story throughout time. Do an image search for "David versus Goliath" and you'll see oil paintings, wood engravings, wall mosaics, marble sculptures, stained-glass windows, and cartoon illustrations of a mythically large soldier towering over a scantily clad tween in a barren wasteland. Some works are recent; many are at least a thousand years old. For generations, these images have shaped society's understanding of what happened in the Valley of Elah. And for a good reason.

Before we can read texts for ourselves, we learn from the stories we hear and the images we see. This has always been true for children singing about Father Abraham and watching Bible-based cartoons, but only within the last few generations have most adults been literate and able to read the Bible for themselves and in their native languages. In 1900, barely 20 percent of the world's population over the age of fourteen could read. In the 1950s, literacy began to increase rapidly, reaching 42 percent in 1960 and 70 percent in 1983. Today, global literacy is 87 percent, and developed nations are over 99 percent.[2] Likewise, complete Bible translations now exist in the native languages of 80 percent of the world's population, and 97 percent have at least some Scripture available to them.[3]

When we are taught from a young age that the ancient world looked a certain way or that the Bible says something that maybe it doesn't actually say, then we subconsciously add those artistic images and traditional assumptions to the words as we read them. The world has told us that young David fought giant Goliath in a dusty desert, so that's what we imagine when we read 1 Samuel 17—even though David was an adult, Goliath is never called a giant, and the Valley of Elah was and is beautifully fertile in the spring.

### How "Great" Was Goliath?

Ignoring thousands of years' worth of the world's illustrations and interpretations, what does the text of 1 Samuel 17 actually describe? Let's start with the man whose popular reputation is more mythical than scriptural:

> And a champion went out from the camp of the Philistines, named Goliath, from Gath, whose height was six cubits and a span. He had a bronze helmet on his head, and he was armed with a coat

of mail, and the weight of the coat was five thousand shekels of bronze. And he had bronze armor on his legs and a bronze javelin between his shoulders. Now the staff of his spear was like a weaver's beam, and his iron spearhead weighed six hundred shekels; and a shield-bearer went before him. (vv. 4–7)

Here Goliath's height is counted as "six cubits and a span." All good Sunday school kids know this translates to almost ten feet tall. What a giant! The problem is, not every ancient text of 1 Samuel 17:4 states "six," and too many English translations don't inform readers that Goliath was more likely "four cubits and a span," which is closer to seven feet tall. Why the discrepancy?

### The Hebrew Bible's Two Primary Texts

As I alluded to in the previous chapter, the words of the Hebrew Bible have been preserved in two distinct versions: a Hebrew version, as one would expect, called the Masoretic Text (MT) and a Greek translation called the Septuagint (LXX). You may have noticed those abbreviations in the footnotes of your favorite Bible translation, but do you know the history and legend packed into those few letters?

The MT is named after the Masoretes, a group of Jewish scribes who lived in exclusive communities between the sixth and tenth centuries CE. They worked to standardize the way scribes copied the sacred texts, adding vowel symbols and cantillation marks so readers would know how to pronounce words that until then had only contained consonants. The oldest-known complete copy of the Masoretic Text is the Leningrad Codex, a book created in 1008 CE and named after the city in which it is housed. It can be viewed at the National Library of Russia in St. Petersburg, which was called Leningrad between 1924 and 1991. If you can't get to Russia, then consider picking up a copy of the *Biblia Hebraica Stuttgartensia*, a typeset and annotated version of the Leningrad Codex that is the basis of most modern translations of the Old Testament and is required reading for students of biblical Hebrew.

The development of the LXX might be more legendary than historical. The story goes that around 250 BCE, King Ptolemy II of Egypt wanted to have a copy of every book in the world translated into Greek and placed in his library. He had his royal librarian write a letter to Eleazar, the high priest in Jerusalem, asking that he assemble six elders from each of the twelve tribes of Israel and send them to Alexandria with the Torah. Upon arrival, all seventy-two were individually cloistered for seventy-two days in the Lighthouse of Alexandria, which was only thirty years old at the time but is among the Seven Wonders of the World today. When the men emerged, each had produced exactly the same translation as the others—seventy-two identical but individual translations! They read the translation to the Egyptian Jews at the court, of which there were many following the Babylonian exile three hundred years earlier. Ptolemy was so impressed that he sent the men back to Jerusalem with gifts for themselves and their high priest, Eleazar.

The Septuagint, a word that derives from the Latin word for "seventy," was a miraculous document because of what it did, even if it lacked miraculous origins. About one hundred years before it was translated, Alexander the Great had conquered everything between his native Macedonia and modern-day Pakistan, so all national languages were changing to Greek. Many Jews inside and outside of Judaea no longer spoke their ancestral language of Hebrew, so the Septuagint was crucial in bringing the Hebrew Scriptures to Jews and non-Jews throughout the Roman Empire.

The Septuagint was also crucial to the development of the early Christian church. It was obviously in use by Jesus and the apostles because its versions of the Hebrew Scriptures are quoted roughly three hundred times all over the New Testament. It made it possible for Jesus's mission to bring all people—not just the Jews—into His Father's family because everyone could read or hear Scriptures in the language they spoke. The translation may not be a perfect word-for-word version of the Masoretic Text (which was still at least nine hundred years in the future), but its creation by Jews in a pagan nation for use by everyone in their known world mirrors God's redemptive work and, I think, indicates the translation process and timing were God-inspired.

### The Importance of the Dead Sea Scrolls

Wherever the "old" Greek translation and the "new" Hebrew transcription disagree, scholars have debated if the accurate word was literally lost in translation or was lost during an extra millennium of copying. Thankfully, many of the discrepancies between the MT and LXX can be solved with context clues, but in the case of Goliath's height, we don't have other biblical passages to help translators and readers.

What the world needed was a third source, and it was found in 1947 when Bedouin shepherds discovered the most famous collection of scrolls in the world. Seven scrolls in one of the caves at Qumran led to international excavations of the area and the discovery of thousands of scroll fragments and a few complete scrolls. The texts, which were well preserved thanks to the arid and salty air on the coast of the Dead Sea, contained all of the Hebrew Bible (excepting Esther and Nehemiah), the Deuterocanon, and many of the scribes' own writings.

Why are these old pieces of parchment, papyrus, and copper so important? Because some of the Dead Sea Scrolls are more than one thousand years older than the Masoretic Text and are almost the same as the Masoretic Text. In places where the Dead Sea Scrolls and the Masoretic Text disagree, the Dead Sea Scrolls usually agree with the Septuagint.[4] Goliath's height is a great example of this. In the younger Masoretic Text of the Hebrew Bible, Goliath was almost ten feet tall; in the older Greek Septuagint text, he was almost seven feet tall. Which is correct? The Dead Sea Scrolls—specifically the Samuel Scrolls—answered this question.

The book of Samuel (which is one book in the ancient texts, not two as our Bibles print it today) was found in four parts among two different caves at Qumran. The Goliath account appears in a collection called 4Q51, and his height is written on Plate 1097, Fragment 2.[5] The Dead Sea Scroll agrees with the Septuagint—his height was "four cubits and a span."

I was surprised to realize that the Bible itself—no matter which translation or text—never actually calls Goliath a giant. He is described as a tall, strong, fearsome warrior, but there is nothing aside from the Masoretic Text to indicate that he lived at the top of a beanstalk, owned a blue ox named Babe, or sold frozen and canned vegetables. But what about the other warriors from his hometown of Gath? Were other Gittites giants?

### Were Goliath's Neighbors Greater?

According to most English translations of 2 Samuel 21:15–21, several Philistine fighters from Gath—but not Goliath himself—were "sons of the giant." The Hebrew word that our translations render as "giant" is *rapha*, and it simply means "great"—greatness in stature, strength, skill, wealth, power, or crispy frosted cereal production is not specified. It is likely that Rapha was actually the father's name and should not be translated but transliterated, as it is in the Berean Study Bible, the New International Version, and The Voice Bible, and as most other English translations footnote it. Archaeological work at Gath supports this idea because "all Philistine skeletal remains discovered so far have shown absolutely no evidence that the people were larger or different from normal-sized people."[6] Giant bones may still be out there waiting to be found, but recent discoveries agree that the city's inhabitants were of normal size.

The Philistine city of Gath is a modern archaeological site called Tel es-Safi, halfway between the Mediterranean port city of Ashkelon and Jerusalem. It has been continuously occupied since the fifth millennium BCE. Gath was in the middle of an important ancient trade route, so the city was large, wealthy, and strategically important to all conquering empires of the ancient world. Because it was sieged and destroyed several times, a lot of material culture remains in the dirt. Archaeologists have been able to reconstruct the daily lives of Gath's first-millennium-BCE citizens by the tools, weapons, pottery, art, and buildings they left behind.

During the 2019 excavation season at Gath, archaeologists unexpectedly uncovered a new layer of civilization that they date to the eleventh century BCE, roughly when David would have killed Goliath. All of the buildings in that layer were made from significantly larger materials than later structures. Building stones were up to two meters long instead of the usual half meter, and the city itself had a footprint twice the size of most of its contemporary neighbors. Imagine if all of the houses in a neighborhood had their red bricks replaced by gray cinderblocks while maintaining the same square footage. The change in materials would be noticeable, but no Titans would have been necessary during construction.

The size differences may indicate that the older Philistines building this eleventh-century city were retaining the architectural traditions of the civilizations from whom they came. What they built was alien to the Israelites in the sense that it was from another culture, not another species.

### The Philistines' Origins

Gath and other Philistine sites have taught us a lot about how Israel's enemy lived, but until recently, Egyptian artifacts told us more about who they were. Near the Valley of the Kings is Medinet Habu, the mortuary temple of Rameses III. Its stone walls are filled with hieroglyphic inscriptions—as are most Egyptian temples and tombs—but this one has unique artistic portrayals of a great sea battle against a group of marauding invaders whom scholars since the end of the nineteenth century have called the "Sea Peoples." These were nine distinct groups of people from the western and eastern Mediterranean, the Aegean, and maybe even Cyprus. They were fierce warriors whose conquests of Egyptian and Canaanite cities brought the Late Bronze Age to an end around 1200 BCE.[7]

The Sea Peoples attacked Egypt twice, just after the death of Rameses the Great when Egypt was still the most powerful empire in the world. Five groups attacked by land in 1207 BCE when Merneptah was pharaoh; six groups attacked by land and sea in 1177 BCE when Rameses III was pharaoh. One of the groups who attacked Rameses III was the Peleset; most scholars agree they were the Philistines. Egyptian records state that the Sea Peoples were thoroughly conquered, but the aftermath tells a different story. Egypt's economy and government were permanently weakened by the conflicts, and the surviving Sea Peoples settled just north of Egypt in cities along the Mediterranean coast. Their warrior culture endured, and for hundreds of years they would be frequently hired by Egypt as mercenaries.

For decades scholars guessed the Sea Peoples (and particularly the Philistines) were from the Aegean because of the similarities between Philistine and Aegean material culture. In the ground, archaeologists can see when the Philistines landed in formerly Canaanite cities because there is evidence of architecture and pottery styles changing.[8]

As science has advanced and given archaeologists powerful tools such as carbon 14 dating and DNA testing, the Philistines' origins have become less mysterious. In 2016, during the final year of excavation at Tel Ashkelon, a large Philistine cemetery was discovered with enough DNA in the bones to test. Just as popular DNA testing kits tell users the origins of their recent and ancient ancestors, Ashkelon's dig directors learned the homeland of those particular Philistines' progenitors were Mediterranean and Aegean islands.[9]

Tradition, Scripture, biblical archaeology, and Egyptology all agree that the Philistines were mighty warriors with technologically advanced weapons and armor. The Egyptians depict the Sea Peoples (including the Peleset) as wearing distinctive feathered headdresses and carrying round shields. Their boats were unique, they used three-man chariots in battle, and they warred as merce-naries for Egypt and other paying clients. Their arrival began the decline of the Egyptian Empire and ended the New Kingdom era in Egypt, just as it marked the end of the Bronze Age. The uniquely large architecture at Gath—combined with the Philistines' general reputation as fierce warriors—could have started the tradition that Goliath was a giant even though Scripture doesn't call him one.

## How "Small" Was David?

So if Goliath and his fellow Gittites weren't the mythically large giants of our Sunday school flannel boards, Saturday morning cartoons, and fifteenth-century artwork, then are we right to en-vision David as the squeaky-voiced, nearly naked tween in those depictions?

The popular image of David as young and gentle—as a shep-herd boy with a fuzzy lamb slung over his narrow shoulders—begins with his status inside his own family. David was indeed the youngest of Jesse's sons (1 Sam. 17:14), but just because someone is the most recently born does not mean he has eternal youth. David's birth order is mentioned in the biblical text because in the ancient Near East, customs dictated that a family's oldest son would inherit the father's fortune, blessing, and status. As the youngest son, David was born to be unremarkable. No one would have expected he could become any sort of leader because wealth, power, and prestige were culturally inherited and not often personally earned.

Our Bible translations go on to tell us that Goliath saw David as "a youth, ruddy and good-looking" (v. 42), but the Hebrew word translated as "youth" has a range of meaning, from "child" to "young man." The translation of the word must consider the broader context of the passage and the claims within the narra-tive. David's own statements about himself to King Saul make it obvious that he was a fully grown, strong man.

When a lion or a bear came and took a lamb out of the flock, I went out after it and struck it, and delivered the lamb from its mouth; and when it arose against me, I caught it by its beard, and struck and killed it. Your servant has killed both lion and bear; and this uncircumcised Philistine will be like one of them, seeing he has defied the armies of the living God. . . . The LORD, who delivered me from the paw of the lion and from the paw of the bear, He will deliver me from the hand of this Philistine. (vv. 34–37)

It is hard to imagine any man—much less an adolescent—wrestling four-hundred-pound wild predators to their deaths, but that's what David put on his résumé. He was advertising his strength, agility, and gumption as he asked King Saul to appoint him Israel's champion in single combat against a professional warrior.

The stakes were high. In the ancient world, opposing armies would sometimes elect to determine the winner of a battle based on single combat. Each side would choose a champion, and the winner's army would "take all" from the loser's army. We have epic stories of these confrontations in many cultures. In ancient Egypt, the Tale of Sanehat (nineteenth century BCE) describes an Egyptian expatriate felling an armored Syrian champion with an arrow to his neck. The ancient Greek epic *Iliad* has two stories of single combat: Mycenaean king Menelaus versus Trojan prince Paris, and demigod Achilles versus Trojan prince Hector. As the Bible describes, David would be fighting against a professional wearing full Mycenaean-style battle dress, including a bronze helmet, coat of mail, leg guards, javelin, and curved sword. But how could David—a common civilian—compete?

## Consider King Henry VIII

Whenever I teach about Goliath's size, someone inevitably points to the text of 1 Samuel 17:5–7 and says, "But look how heavy his equipment was!" Scholars estimate that Goliath's armor weighed about 126 pounds and his spearhead weighed about 15 pounds. (These are estimates because biblical weights are just as uncertain as biblical lengths.)

In 1520, Henry VIII was six feet, two inches tall and had many suits of armor. His foot combat armor weighed 94 pounds and was made of carbon steel.[10] Even if Goliath was "only" six feet, seven inches tall, his armor would have been larger and therefore heavier. The material of his equipment—bronze—was also about 10 percent heavier than steel, which had not yet been invented. Yes, this Philistine warrior's outfit and weapons were heavy—too heavy for most of us to even put on!—but they were not "giant" in scale.

---

In the ancient Near East, sheep were domesticated for their meat and hides, but they were highly valued for their wool. They needed to be tended constantly and carefully by shepherds because they were easy prey for wild animals and lacked natural defense mechanisms like an ibex's prominent horns, agility, and speed. To protect his flock, a shepherd such as David needed keen eyesight to see animals lurking, speed and courage to confront a charging predator, and skill with a staff and sling.

The sling was not a y-shaped stick with a rubber band tied to it. Archaeologists have found stone projectiles for slings from as early as the Neolithic period, but the slings themselves are a rarer find. Each would have been biodegradable, made of a large cloth or leather pocket connected to two ropes. The user would place a stone in the pocket, hold the ends of the ropes in one hand, twirl the sling above his head, and release one of the ropes. The half-pound stone would then shoot forward at speeds up to 150 miles per hour. The stones were often made of flint, could be round or almond-shaped, and were carried in a shoulder bag. Mastery of the sling took time and practice, but a skilled slinger was valuable as a shepherd and a soldier.

On the surface, it is still strange that King Saul should appoint a man he'd never met and with zero combat training to fight for the fate of all Israelites. Maybe after forty days of facing off against the Philistines in the valley, Saul was just ready to be finished. Or maybe he recognized that as a shepherd, David had spent his life as a lone champion fighting off stronger opponents with a tactical weapon—a sling.

In Judges 20:16, the Bible describes an elite group of seven hundred left-handed Benjaminites who "could sling a stone at a hair's breadth and not miss." The power of the sling in the hand of a practiced thrower was legendary in Israel's history and in Saul's own tribe of Benjamin. The sling would continue to be used effectively in battle for hundreds of years, as slingers are memorialized next to archers in the Lachish Reliefs, Assyria's depiction of their victory over Judah's city of Lachish in 701 BCE.[11]

David's skills as a shepherd easily translated to the battlefield. In the chapter following Goliath's death, King Saul "set him over the men of war" (18:5), that is, he made David a commander in Israel's army. Immediately David was hailed as a conquering hero and joined the royal household—first as the best friend of the crown prince, Jonathan, and then as the husband of Saul's daughter, Michal. But David quickly became Saul's enemy instead of his ally, so we learn that David was also politically savvy, making alliances with the Philistines while he worked to bring all of Israel's tribes together and to conquer other nations—including those Philistines!

---

## David's Cleverest Wife

David's skill with the sling gets one more meaningful shout-out in Scripture. While fighting with Saul to become the king of the twelve tribes of Israel, David visits Carmel. There he meets Abigail, the wife of a foolish man named Nabal, whom David would soon marry.

It seems that Abigail was as smart as her husband was dumb, and she uses her words to charm her king. She predicts David's victory over King Saul by hearkening back to the events in the Valley of

Elah: "A man has risen to pursue you and seek your life, but the life of my lord shall be bound in the bundle of the living with the LORD your God; and *the lives of your enemies He shall sling out, as from the pocket of a sling*" (1 Sam. 25:29).

David didn't just marry Abigail for her beauty and brains; she brought with her Nabal's wealth and influence over the Calebites. She was key to gaining their support for David's kingship, and at Hebron he would soon be anointed king over the house of Judah (2 Sam. 2:4), of which the Calebites were a part.

---

David versus Goliath is not a stand-alone story but a single episode in the rise of the man after God's own heart (1 Sam. 13:14) from an obscure birth to becoming the unifier of the twelve tribes and the great king of His nation, Israel.

## Conclusion

The exaggerated ways the tradition has depicted both men—Goliath as a mythical giant and David as a skinny lad—have resulted in a well-used and sometimes trite metaphor designed to explain the success of a weakling in the face of impossible odds. The all-too-familiar "miracle" of David's win over a superhuman can obscure important details of the story as it focuses on the outcome and not on the ways God was preparing a young man for his great future.

God had gifted David with a set of skills that made him able not only to win a battle but later to conquer and rule a kingdom. He was smart enough to avoid wearing ill-fitting, restrictive armor; he was strong enough to carry five sizable stones (not just pebbles) and sling one with the speed of a bullet train and the accuracy of an actual bullet; he was agile enough to evade the skilled jabs of a seasoned warrior; and, most importantly, he was faithful enough to his God to fight confidently in His name when others were afraid. This wasn't a battle of weak versus strong or small versus big or even young versus old. It was an example of how God defies expectations.

God has a habit of choosing underdogs and gifting the unexceptional to do the work of His kingdom. In the ancient Near East, customs dictated that a man's oldest son inherited his fortune and blessing, but not in God's family. He chose Isaac over Ishmael, Jacob over Esau, Judah over Reuben, David over all his older brothers, Solomon over Adonijah . . . and the list goes on. God takes time to prepare the ill-equipped to do great things in His name. He consistently bucks humanity's systems so that we can recognize His work and praise Him for it.

# King Solomon's Disappearance

Within a grove of trees, tucked tightly between a middle school and a primary school, my hometown's small public library once sat. The children's section inside it was magical: perfectly square with grass-colored carpet, colorful bookcases stacked to the ceiling (which looked thirty feet high from my perspective), and a librarian ready to run a ladder around the space to pull down any book I requested. The section I always investigated first contained the Great Illustrated Classics, which are abridged versions of novels and fairy tales with full-page pen-and-ink illustrations every few pages. Over the years I read every one of the sixty-six books in the series, and three of them are now in my own home waiting to be read by the next generation. They sit quietly inside the "magical" cabinet I keep stocked with coloring books and games for when my nieces and nephews visit. Someday soon they will be able to reach in themselves, but for now I get to play librarian (and artist and game master!) in residence.

One of those abridged classics is *King Solomon's Mines*, which was first published in 1885. The legend goes that author H. Rider

Haggard accepted his brother's challenge to write a novel that would be more popular than Robert Louis Stevenson's *Treasure Island*, and he did just that in only six weeks. The adventures of the book's fictional narrator and central character, Allan Quatermain, would go on to feature in eighteen books and stories, creating the popular "lost world" genre of novels. Without Allan Quatermain we might not have famous fantasy adventurers such as Indiana Jones and Lara Croft or the worlds created by H. G. Wells, Arthur Conan Doyle, and Michael Crichton.

In the unabridged version of *King Solomon's Mines*, the English elephant hunter, Quatermain, is hired by two men to find an English aristocrat who has been lost in Africa while looking for King Solomon's diamond mines in the fictional "Suliman Mountains up to the north-west of the Mashukulumbwe country."[1] Following a map given to Quatermain by a Portuguese explorer, the men have adventures in areas representing all of Africa's physical regions, with the help of natives who are more stereotypical than historical in their characterizations. They are eventually led to Solomon's treasure chamber, which is a stalactite cave filled with elephant ivory, gold pieces "with what looked like Hebrew characters stamped upon them" in wooden boxes, and three stone boxes containing "millions of pounds' worth of diamonds."[2] What follows is a Spielberg- and Lucas-worthy series of scenes in which the African guide traps the men inside the mountain, leaving them to find a different, more treacherous escape. In the end, Allan Quatermain agrees to return to England to enjoy a wealthy retirement thanks to Solomon's treasures that had never made it to the king in Israel.

The legend of Solomon's mines—like much of what we will explore in this chapter—is based on a fictional idea that has captured imaginations for well over a century. However, there is only one mention of mines in the Hebrew Bible (Job 28:1–2), and that reference has no connection to Israel's wealthy kings or Africa's native diamonds, ivory, and gold. What the Bible does tell us about Solomon—that he was the wealthiest and wisest man in the world (1 Kings 10:23), was a developer of God's first temple and multiple fortified cities, and had wives from many surrounding nations—leads us to the reasonable assumption that he would have supported international mining operations and had an overflowing treasury of his own. But there is no reason to put those two concepts together, focus on the "shiny objects" out in the world, and miss what Scripture does tell us about one of Israel's greatest kings: He was a prolific builder and a wise ruler—with a giant soft spot for foreign women.

## Solomon the Builder

Tangentially related to the nineteenth-century stories of Solomon's fictional mines is the Bible's real mention of the stonemasons he employed at quarries in the region. King Solomon may be best known as a builder—or maybe more of a developer, as we would say today—of Israel's greatest Iron Age cities and Jerusalem's first temple. He organized a workforce by conscripting Israelite men to day labors (1 Kings 5:13–14), hired talented superintendents to run the work (v. 16), and acquired the highest-quality materials from surrounding nations (v. 6). I doubt he ever handled a chisel or set a cornerstone himself.

### Solomon's Temple

Solomon's story begins in 1 Kings 1, when his father, King David, agrees to give the throne not to his oldest living son, Adonijah—as everyone, including Adonijah and David's military leaders, expected—but to his tenth son, Solomon. Reams of paper have been filled with theories as to why Solomon was chosen: Maybe all of his older brothers were dead except for Adonijah, whom he will have killed in the next chapter. Maybe Adonijah disqualified himself by being anointed prior to his father's death. Maybe David wasn't in his right mind at the end of his life and Bathsheba hoodwinked him into making her the queen mother. Maybe this was a Joseph situation in which David loved Bathsheba more than his other wives and therefore favored her son.

Kings doesn't really answer the why question, but the Chronicler's retelling of the story does. God Himself said to David, "Behold, a son shall be born to you, who shall be a man of rest; and I will give him rest from all his enemies all around. His name shall be Solomon, for I will give peace and quietness to Israel in his days. He shall build a house for My name, and he shall be My son, and I will be his Father; and I will establish the throne of his kingdom over Israel forever" (1 Chron. 22:9–10). After decades of wars fought by Saul and David to unify the tribes into one nation under one king, God would elevate a man of peace who would develop the nation and God's temple. Solomon's name is derived from the Hebrew root word transliterated as *SLM*, which means "whole, complete" and often has the connotation of "peace," as peace only comes when there is no division. Solomon's reign would be a "complete" forty years known for being a time of growth, wealth, and peace within Israel and with neighboring nations.

Even a quick skim of Samuel and Kings will show that Israel's history is one of almost constant struggle: a struggle to unite, a struggle to divide, and struggles against big bad foreign powers. Solomon's reign breaks that mold, and the chapters devoted to him after he has secured his throne are mostly lists of his building accomplishments, with a few colorful anecdotes sprinkled here and there.

Everyone knows Solomon's most famous building project was God's first temple in Jerusalem. Unfortunately, there is zero archaeological evidence of the structure, and remnants of the building are unlikely to ever be found. In 586 BCE, Nebuchadnezzar led his Babylonian army to destroy Jerusalem. The buildings, including the temple, were razed and the land left open to the elements until the Jews were allowed to return from their exile in 538 BCE. Today's visitors to the Western Wall are praying at the remains of a two-thousand-year-old retaining wall built and backfilled by King Herod to enlarge and protect the space surrounding the second temple, which was initially built under the direction of Ezra and Nehemiah. That temple was similarly destroyed by the Romans in 70 CE, but they left the Temple Mount in place.

Although Solomon's temple is long gone, we have a good idea of how it may have looked. The biblical descriptions of the building, its furniture, and its decorations are thorough, and in the places where Hebrew words may be unknown or descriptions might not make sense, we can look to artifacts discovered in surrounding cities and cultures. In northwest Syria, there was once a beautiful example of a stone temple that largely matched the description of Israel's. It contained a vestibule, an outer sanctuary, a square holy of holies, a side chamber, and an entry porch with two columns. Its floor plan helped Bible readers and illustrators to "see" what Scripture described. Sadly, the temple at Ain Dara was destroyed by Turkish forces on January 22, 2018,[3] but images of its cherubim carvings, giant footprints, and basalt foundation stones have survived. Other stone temples with architectural similarities— although not as many as at Ain Dara—are still safe at Tel Tayinat in Turkey and Moza in Israel.[4]

### Solomon's Cities

Although not as famous as his temple, three of Solomon's biggest building projects have been located, excavated, and in some areas restored for visitors to enjoy. Megiddo, Hazor, and Gezer were Canaanite cities on popular trading routes that had been destroyed during the thirteenth century. Archaeologists found that the cities were revitalized—and fortified—during the tenth century, around the time when Solomon would have been on the throne (1 Kings 9:15–19).

The walls that Solomon had built to fortify those cities were not just courses of stone block as you might imagine. They were *casemate walls*, a type of construction that was cheaper, stronger, more useful, and longer lasting. A casemate was formed when two parallel walls that doubly enclosed a city were connected at intervals by perpendicular sections of wall. The cells (casemates) formed within the two parallel walls could be filled in with rubble for extra protection, or they could be used for storage.

Such thick walls couldn't be protected by a simple swinging gate like those we use to secure our properties today. Gates were often buildings with four to six chambers, with half the rooms on one side of a passageway and half on the other side. In those chambers, the men of the city would meet to decide civic matters, such as whether or not Boaz could marry King David's great-grandmother, Ruth (Ruth 4:1–12). Adjacent to the gate would be the town square where merchants would sell their produce and wares, so it was important that the corridor between the chambers of a gate be wide enough to allow cargo inside—but narrow enough to keep the gate defensible.[5] And these cities needed to be defensible, especially Megiddo.

Thanks to corroborating evidence from other nations' records, the battle timeline for Megiddo can be rather easily constructed. The first battle in the world's recorded history happened at Megiddo: Egyptian Pharaoh Thutmose III fought a Canaanite coalition there in 1468 BCE, taking the city after a seven-month siege. Pharaoh Merneptah tried to take it in 1220 BCE, and then Pharaoh Shoshenq I (whom the Bible calls Shishak) attacked in 924 BCE. The Assyrian king Tiglath Pilesar III captured Megiddo and made it the capital of a district that included Galilee. And in 609 BCE, Egypt's pharaoh Necho II took it back from Assyria and killed the southern king Josiah, as reported in 2 Kings 23:29.[6]

Contemporary battles have also been fought there. In 1917, General Edmund Allenby fought the Ottoman Turks at Megiddo and won control of the Jezreel Valley. At the end of World War I, he became known as "Lord Allenby of Megiddo."[7] Modern-day Israel has fought battles there in 1948, 1967, and 1973, and it has been foretold that the world's penultimate battle will one day take place there: "They gathered them together to the place which in Hebrew is called Har-Magedon [Mount Megiddo]" (Rev. 16:16 NASB). That one little mention has spawned two thousand years' worth of speculations about the end times. There is no consensus on what the future holds, and I seriously doubt an ancient stone tablet will be found there with battle plans and dates.

Excavations are continuing at Megiddo, Hazor, and Gezer (the city given to Solomon's Egyptian wife by her father in 1 Kings 9:16), and certainly we have more to learn from those cities about Israel's past. One can only hope that somewhere in the cities' walls or palaces or maybe even stables there will be a stele. During the tenth century, kings from Egypt and Mesopotamia were famous for recording—and maybe embellishing—their accomplishments on stone. That is how we know so much about Megiddo's bloody history from other cultures. To date, no such stone has been found with Solomon's name on it—not in Israel or any surrounding nation. The only evidence we have of him is the biblical account and much later stories about him from other cultures.

## The Low Chronology

Not everyone accepts Israel's historical record—as recorded in the Hebrew Bible—as historical. Because there is no extrabiblical, universally accepted physical evidence of Saul, David, or Solomon, some scholars argue that they never existed as kings of Israel. This is true of the current and longtime excavator at Tel Megiddo, Israel Finkelstein.[8]

The Low Chronology is a revised timeline for ancient Israel that cuts the first three kings out of history, so that the timeline of ancient Israel moved straight from the period of the judges into the divided monarchy, with the asterisk that if David did exist, then he was just a judge and not a king. According to this theory, activities that the Bible attributes to those three were actually accomplished by the early northern and southern kings.

If you are ever able to visit Tel Megiddo, then you will be taught the Low Chronology as historical fact. In the visitors' center, Solomon is not credited as the Iron Age city's designer and builder. The northern king Ahab (husband to "bad girl" Jezebel) is.

## Solomon the Author

As I began drafting this chapter, I asked my husband David what comes to his mind when Solomon is mentioned. His answer surprised me: "When I was growing up, my brother and I would go to my Amish grandmother's house several times each week and study the Bible. She would help us memorize verses and explain words and concepts that were too challenging for elementary readers. But she had one rule: Never read Song of Solomon. Which, of course, pushed me to binge-read the book in search of what was forbidden! I didn't understand what the big deal was. All of the metaphorical language went straight over my head."

Tradition credits Solomon with authorship of three books in the Bible: Proverbs, Ecclesiastes, and Song of Songs. In Christian Bibles, the three books are printed next to each other because of their traditional connection to Solomon, but not in the Hebrew Bible. All three books are part of the third section of the Hebrew Bible, called the *Ketuvim*, which means "writings." It is the last section and follows the Torah and the Prophets. It is also the youngest and most diverse section, encompassing poetry, philosophical reflections, retellings of history, and short narratives.

The tradition that Solomon wrote these books is not exactly scriptural. No one is credited with Ecclesiastes, and Solomon's name is not even mentioned in the book. Both Proverbs and Song of Songs mention Solomon in their first verses but not in a byline.

Proverbs is a collection of nine distinct writings, only three of which mention Solomon. In the Hebrew, it is easier to tell that Proverbs is an anthology of several collections of sayings. Some of these are directly attributed to their authors (such as Agur the son of Jakeh in 30:1); others were written or collected by an unidentified "teacher" of young men. Proverbs 31 says it is the collected sayings of King Lemuel's mother as told to her son. But because the book begins "The proverbs of Solomon," some readers carry over the idea that Solomon was the author of not only those three sections (beginning in 1:1, 10:1, and 25:1) but of the entire book.

But even those three sections are not "by Solomon" but "of Solomon," just as seventy-three psalms are "of David." The word "of" is a simple preposition that means something like "inspired by," "written for," or even "commissioned by." It does not mean "by" in the sense that this book is "by Amanda Hope Haley"; that would require a different Hebrew preposition. Maybe the kings originated the credited psalms and proverbs, but based on the language, they did not sit down and put pen to parchment. Proverbs and Psalms were likely compiled from oral traditions and edited after the exile during the fourth century BCE.[9] The language supports that date, as does the setting of Proverbs, which is a school. Young men would have gathered in a small group to learn from an older man, usually a scribe, but that practice did not begin in the region of ancient Israel until after the exile. As mentioned in the Bible, children were taught by their parents prior to 586 BCE. Women taught their daughters daily household tasks; fathers—be they shepherds, farmers, scribes, or kings—taught their vocations to their sons. Institutionalized education as described in Proverbs was first witnessed by the Judahites as they lived among the Babylonians, who had schools as early as the third millennium BCE.[10]

Song of Songs is a slightly different case. The first verse, from which most biblical books take their titles, can be literally translated as "Song of songs which is to/for/of Solomon." In Hebrew, when a word is repeated as "song" is here, it means that the repeated word is simply the best! The Hebrew is telling the reader that this is the greatest song of all time, just as Nebuchadnezzar and Artaxerxes were each described as a "king of kings" of their respective countries (Ezek. 26:7; Ezra 7:12), and Jesus is "King of kings and Lord of lords" for all humanity (1 Tim. 6:15).

Only English translations of the Christian canon call the book Song of Solomon; it was an early flawed translation that was later copied by the King James Version and many subsequent

117

translations simply for tradition's sake. Including the superscription, Solomon is mentioned in the book ten times, either by name or simply as "king," but he is not a character or a singer. His glorious reign is the backdrop to the beautiful love story between the unnamed man and woman.

## Solomon the Lover

Solomon may not have written Song of Songs, but the fact that many of us were taught he is the unnamed male lover in the song fits with one well-known fact about the man: "King Solomon loved many foreign women, as well as the daughter of Pharaoh: women of the Moabites, Ammonites, Edomites, Sidonians, and Hittites—from the nations of whom the LORD had said to the children of Israel, 'You shall not intermarry with them, nor they with you. Surely they will turn away your hearts after their gods.' Solomon clung to these in love. And he had seven hundred wives, princesses, and three hundred concubines; and his wives turned away his heart" (1 Kings 11:1–3). In short, he was a ladies' man (as we might say today), and that desire for human affection would split ancient Israel in two.

### Seven Hundred Princesses (and Three Hundred Concubines)

When I read about Solomon's harem of one thousand women, I can't help but remember the scene of Anna Leonowens meeting the many wives, concubines, and children of King Mongkut's harem in the 1956 film version of Rodgers and Hammerstein's *The King and I*. Yul Brynner (during the same year he played DeMille's pharaoh) stands proudly as his family parades in front of their new English teacher, expecting Anna to be extra-impressed by his twin sons amid the pomp and circumstance of his family's presentation to her.[11]

This fictional story, which was loosely based on the interactions between the real Anna and the King of Siam from 1862 to 1867, gives us a glimpse of the role of royal women in Eastern courts. Quite simply, they were viewed as property as recently as the nineteenth century. In the film, the newest member of the king's harem, a woman named Tuptim, is "given" to him by the Prince of Burma. The woman loves one of her own countrymen and is miserable at the palace, but her feelings do not matter. For thousands of years, women had married foreign rulers to seal international treaties and bear sons who would forever link the countries in friendship. (At least that was the idea. It didn't always work out well!)

King Solomon's harem of one thousand women was substantially larger than King Mongkut's thirty-nine, but the intention was likely the same. Solomon's own father, David, had multiple wives who seem to have been strategically chosen based on their tribe or land of origin. His first wife, Michal, was the daughter of King Saul and gave him direct access to the throne. Over the years, he married Abigail (whose first husband was a Calebite leader), Ahinoam (who may have previously been Saul's wife according to 1 Sam. 14:50), and Maachah (the daughter of the king of Geshur), among others. The total number of David's wives and concubines is not recorded, and his reasons for marrying differed slightly from Solomon's. David was pulling together all of Israel's tribes under one king, while Solomon was building diplomatic connections with foreign kings.

Of his one thousand wives and concubines, only two are identified and only one is named: the daughter of the pharaoh (1 Kings 9:16) and Naamah, the Ammonite mother of Solomon's successor (14:21). But the regions the women came from—Egypt, Moab, Ammon, Edom, Sidon (Phoenicia), and Heth (Anatolia)—bordered Solomon's kingdom and were ancient and recent enemies of Israel. Without names and stories about the princesses and concubines, we are left to assume they were political pawns who brought their foreign, pagan traditions with them to Solomon's court.

In the Law, God prohibited His people from intermarrying with several groups, including the Hittites, Moabites, and Ammonites

(Deut. 7:3; 23:3), all who were part of Solomon's harem. After the exile, as Ezra is reflecting on the Israelites' past and present sin, he explains that part of the reason Jerusalem was conquered was because those marriage laws were violated (Ezra 9–10). Solomon, as a man of peace, wasn't wrong to negotiate with foreign leaders. His error was in adopting the pagan traditions, rituals, and gods that his wives brought into his nation and palace (1 Kings 11:1–8).

### One Queen

Not one of Solomon's wives is given the title "queen" in Scripture, but there was one queen with whom he famously interacted: the queen of Sheba. Just before we read about Solomon abandoning right worship of his God, 1 Kings 10 tells us about her state visit. But there might be less in the text than you'd imagine. The Bible says only that she had heard about Solomon's devotion to God, traveled to meet him, exchanged gifts, was impressed by the organization of his court, and talked with him at length.

What is "missing" from the Bible that we might expect to find? An account of her great beauty. A passionate love affair between the two monarchs. Details of the wisdom Solomon shared with her. A son and heir. The location of Sheba. Extrabiblical writings and popular culture have filled in those "gaps" so that we tend to know more about her legend than her person.

The historical queen of Sheba is a mystery, as is the exact location of her kingdom. Historically, geographically, and archaeologically speaking, the kingdom of Sheba has long been identified with Saba, which is just across the Red Sea from Ethiopia in modern-day Yemen. Ethiopia and Saba traded with each other in antiquity, and there is evidence of Saba's influence on Ethiopian culture as early as 800 BCE. Some Ethiopian kings even titled themselves as rulers of Saba, although they don't appear to have actually governed Saba. Today, ancient Saba's capital of Marib is in danger from the Yemeni civil war, meaning archaeological evidence of the city's early rulers may be destroyed before the sites can be excavated.[12]

The location of Sheba conflicts with most of our accepted traditions about the queen herself. *Kebra Nagast*, which translates from Ge'ez as "The Glory of Kings," is a Christian Ethiopian Orthodox text written only seven hundred years ago. Its purpose was "to establish the truth of the origins of the Solomonic dynasty of [Ethiopian] Kings and the current abode of the Ark of the Covenant."[13] According to this book, the queen of Sheba was the queen of Ethiopia. She heard about Solomon's wisdom and wealth from a merchant and decided to visit Jerusalem. While there, Solomon seduced her and impregnated her. On her way back to Ethiopia, the queen birthed Solomon's first son, Menyelek I, who returned to meet his father when he was twenty-two years old. Solomon wanted Menyelek to stay and succeed him as Israel's king, but when Menyelek insisted on returning to his mother, Solomon sent him back with an entourage. Unbeknownst to Menyelek, his companions had taken the ark of the covenant, leaving a replica in the temple. The ark magically transported the group to Aksum, where the queen abdicated her throne in favor of her son.

In many ways, the *Kebra Nagast* reminds me of the Book of Enoch that we referenced in chapter 2. It is a fun read written far too late to have any sort of spiritual authority, but its colorful narratives have infiltrated our culture to the point that Bible readers might subconsciously incorporate its fiction between the lines of God's Word. And like the Book of Enoch, it has us wondering where an ark—this time the ark of the covenant—may be located. Today, the Ethiopian Orthodox Church claims to have the ark of the covenant in Aksum, but no one is allowed to see it. This is one of several traditional theories as to the demise of the ark of the covenant, which we will consider in chapter 9.

## Conclusion

God's declaration that David's line would continue to rule a united Israel was contingent upon one thing: devotion to God. But Solomon allowed himself to be swayed from his dual role as king of Israel and worshiper-in-chief. Near the end of Solomon's life, after he had worshiped the gods of his wives and built sanctuaries for their idols, God told him, "Because you have done this, and have not kept My covenant and My statutes, which I have commanded you, I will surely tear the kingdom away from you and give it to your servant. Nevertheless I will not do it in your days, for the sake of your father David; I will tear it out of the hand of your son. However I will not tear away the whole kingdom; I will give one tribe to your son for the sake of My servant David, and for the sake of Jerusalem which I have chosen" (1 Kings 11:11–13). That is why ancient Israel only had one generation of unity and peace: God kept His promise to David, but Solomon did not keep his promise to God.

Maybe it is by design that we are obsessed with the legend of Solomon, that we look for spectacular evidence of his power that has long been buried beneath the surface. Our legends remind us of the best parts of Solomon as modern scholars doubt his existence.

No amount of wealth or wisdom could make up for abandoning right worship of God. Even though Solomon built the temple and improved Jerusalem, fortified his nation's cities for coming wars, and kept peace with his neighbors, Israel split in two soon after his death because Solomon failed to uphold his own righteous values and instill them in his people or in his son and successor, Rehoboam. His biblical legacy is not in his accomplishments but in the division of Israel caused by his sin. No matter how great our material contributions on this earth, they can disappear when not in step with God's will.

# 8

# Jonah's Whale of a Tale

One summer while I was home from college, I traveled to visit my cousins for a few days. That week the two oldest had participated in their church's annual Vacation Bible School. On Friday night, the event closed with a play, *Jonah and the Whale*, and I had the joy of watching the only other redhead in my family in the title role. Ten-year-old Matt spent thirty minutes as the tortured prophet, brilliantly delivering his lines around a giant papier-mâché whale that took up most of the stage, before sitting inside the fearsome creature to sing a song of lament.

The previous semester I had become deeply familiar with Jonah. My five-member Biblical Hebrew class would gather with our professor at eight o'clock on Monday, Wednesday, and Friday mornings in the refectory for breakfast and translation. We were always tired and a bit silly, so it was good that we were working with Jonah—which is only four chapters long and is itself a bit humorous (but for good reason). So sitting in the audience that hot summer evening, I was both an outwardly proud cousin and a silently obnoxious critic, puffed up with my new knowledge that no whale appears in the book of Jonah.

It is no surprise that Jonah's story ranks highly among VBS curricula builders. The nautical setting of the first two chapters inspires flowing sanctuary decorations, easy-to-make fishing games, seashell-based crafts, and colorful cartoon characters who would be at home in Disney's *Pinocchio* or Pixar's *Finding Nemo*. The brevity of the book means the whole narrative can be taught in four or five days, and the popularized "moral of the story"—that God loves us even when we misbehave—applies to children and adults alike.

But how many adults never go beyond the Saturday morning–cartoon version of Jonah themselves? When our children come home from a fun day of learning about the Bible, do we understand the book well enough to push them beyond entertainment to understanding? The historical background for Jonah's exploits—the coming conquest of Israel's Northern Kingdom—may be too violent for elementary-aged children, but eventually Christians need to encounter the Scripture's complexity to understand its prime place in both Israelite history and early Christian culture.

## Why Was Jonah in Such a Bad Mood?

After King Solomon's death in the tenth century, the United Kingdom of Israel split into the Southern Kingdom, ruling the tribes of Judah and Benjamin and centered in Jerusalem, and the Northern Kingdom, ruling the other ten tribes and eventually centered in Samaria. In the absence of a strong, diplomatic, and wealthy king such as Solomon, both nations spent the following two-plus centuries trading, allying, and fighting with the Egyptian Empire in the south and the Neo-Assyrian Empire in the north and east. The struggles are a primary historical focus in the books of 1 and 2 Kings.

During the eighth century in particular, when Jonah would have lived, the Northern Kingdom found the Neo-Assyrian Empire to be more foe than friend. The Assyrian culture had begun around 2000 BCE, but it reached its height between 911 and 609 as the largest empire the world had seen up until that time. In the 700s, both the Northern and Southern Kingdoms were on Neo-Assyria's hit list, but only the Northern Kingdom would completely fall to them in 722 BCE.

---

### *What Made These Assyrians "Neo"?*

Assyrian culture had several phases of civilization, similar to the Old, Middle, and New Kingdoms of the ancient Egyptian Empire. During the fourth phase of the Assyrian civilization, the people experienced a renaissance and the leaders focused on conquering everyone surrounding them. The empire-building, neighbor-decimating kings have been called "neo" by anthropologists, archaeologists, and historians to distinguish them from their less-domineering ancestors.

Likewise, the aggressive Neo-Babylonian Empire, which would replace the Neo-Assyrians in 612 and conquer the Egyptians in 605, was a second wave of Babylonians who ruled the region until they were conquered by the Persians in 539 BCE. The Old Babylonian Empire, which existed between 1894 and 1595 BCE, had long since faded into history.

---

The conquest of the Northern Kingdom gives us an idea of when Jonah must have had his Mediterranean adventure, which is helpful since the Bible itself does not give many biographical details except that Jonah is the son of Amittai. Outside of the book of Jonah, he is only mentioned one other time in the Hebrew Bible, in 2 Kings 14:25, where we are told he prophesied against the Arameans during the reign of Jeroboam II (786–746 BCE). Those two references give us a window for dating Jonah's travels: 786–722 BCE.

It would be nice to narrow those dates even further, but the book of Jonah does not provide necessary details to do so. If this story had been told in the books of Kings, then we might read the name of the Neo-Assyrian king who heard Jonah's prophecy. But this is not a historical book, so that detail is left out just as the pharaoh goes unnamed in Exodus. The author does not include historical details because either he assumes his readers already know the setting or those facts do not impact the theological message of the book. Or probably both. Thankfully, Assyriology helps today's reader to contextualize Scripture historically and better understand the narrative.

### What Is Assyriology?

Within the field of Near Eastern archaeology, students and professionals often focus their efforts on one region's cultures and languages. People who excavate in and around modern-day Israel are commonly called *biblical archaeologists* because ancient Israel's historical record is largely contained in the Hebrew Bible. Those who explore ancient Egypt's temples and cities and read Egyptian hieroglyphs, hieratic, and demotic are *Egyptologists*. Similarly, scholars of ancient Assyria's many cultures, who all wrote in versions of cuneiform, are called *Assyriologists*. There are obvious overlaps between the specialties because the ancient cultures interacted with each other.

The brave and brilliant souls who choose to study Assyriology commit themselves to learning the languages and dialects written in cuneiform. Around 3200 BCE, scribes in the Sumerian city-state of Uruk first formed clay into wet tablets, pressed wedge-shaped reed styluses into the clay, and then baked the tablets.[1] Different cultures throughout the region employed the same technique over the next three thousand years, although the languages evolved over time and in different locations. (It is similar to how France, England, Spain, Germany, and other nations started with the same alphabet but their languages evolved independently.) Today, thanks to the durability of thick baked clay, there are hundreds of thousands of cuneiform tablets in museums and private collections, with untold numbers still in the ground. Stone stelae, created by chiseling the letters in stone, also abound.

The translation of the cuneiform languages began with the discovery of the Behistun Inscription on a rock cliff at Mount Behistun in Iran.[2] This large bas-relief commissioned by Persian emperor Darius I in 521 BCE measures 15 meters high by 25 meters wide, and it towers 60 meters above the plain—where it couldn't be easily tampered with, but also where it couldn't be easily read! The relief is the longest-known trilingual cuneiform inscription, written in cuneiform script of the Old Persian, Elamite, and Babylonian languages; and just as the Rosetta Stone helped scholars to decipher the ancient Egyptian languages in 1822, this inscription helped to decipher cuneiform in 1857.

The copious records from Sumerian, Assyrian, Babylonian, Persian, and other cultures are the foundation of Assyriology. Around 650 BCE, Assyrian king Ashurbanipal began building a library at Nineveh and collecting as many cuneiform tablets as could be found. That library was discovered by Sir Austen Henry Layard in the 1840s as he excavated the king's Southwest and Northwest Palaces. As more writings were discovered throughout the region, they were collected into the Mesopotamian Chronicles, which contain histories of battles, court records, and letters, but also poetry, myths, and wisdom literature all dating from approximately 1500 to 100 BCE.[3]

### Neo-Assyrian Dominance

So what do all of those records tell us was happening in Neo-Assyria between 786 and 722 BCE that could have infuriated Jonah so much that he initially ignored God's command to call the people to repentance (Jon. 1:2–3)? The short answer is growth and conquest. Under emperors Shalmaneser IV (782–773), Tiglath-Pileser III (745–727), Shalmaneser V (726–722), and the less-famous rulers in between, Neo-Assyria systematically conquered their neighbors and destroyed those societies with policies of total exile and destruction.

During the likely period of Jonah's prophetic work, Neo-Assyria's capital was at Nimrud, near the banks of the Tigris River. Excavations of the site, which lies nearly twenty miles south of modern-day Mosul, Iraq, began under British archaeologist Sir Austen Henry Layard in 1845 and have continued during peacetime to today. At its height, the city was nearly 1.4 square miles and supported seventy-five thousand people. It had multiple palaces and temples, a large library of cuneiform texts, royal tombs, an arsenal, and beautiful artwork. The walls were covered by giant stone relief panels depicting the king, various gods, warfare, and life scenes. *Lamassu*—colossal sculptures of lions or bulls with wings and human heads (which the Bible would call *cherubim*)—are iconic Mesopotamian guardian creatures that would protect entrances to state buildings. Stelae commemorate Neo-Assyrian kings with portraits and cuneiform stories of their conquests. The one thousand Nimrud ivories, the 120 bronze Nimrud bowls, and the more than six hundred pieces of jewelry in the Treasure of Nimrud all attest to the city's wealth and beauty.[4]

After Neo-Assyria conquered the Northern Kingdom in 722 BCE, Sargon II moved the imperial capital from Nimrud to Khorsabad. His son, Sennacherib, moved the capital again—this time to Nineveh, in the modern-day city of Mosul—beginning in 704 BCE. The area's fertile riverbanks had supported human civilization as early as the Neolithic period, and it had grown steadily as successive groups moved in and took advantage of its prime trading location. There, between 701 and 693 BCE, Sennacherib's investment in infrastructure elevated the city from notable regional village to the epicenter of Neo-Assyrian culture. With an area of seven square miles and nearly 150,000 residents, it was the largest city in the world. Inside the massive wall with fifteen gates, he built his Palace Without Rival, encompassing over 1.3 million square feet, which included an immense library of its own. The walls were carved with reliefs of campaigns and Assyrian history, the most famous of which might be his account of the 701 BCE Siege of Lachish (1 Kings 18; 2 Chron. 32). Once again, giant lamassu "guarded" entrances. Many of the palace's treasures were shipped to European museums for exhibition. At the British Museum, reliefs have been displayed so that visitors can imagine themselves inside the palace.[5]

Both Nimrud and Nineveh would be destroyed by the Neo-Babylonian Empire in 612, but their beauty remained the stuff of legends. One of the Seven Wonders of the Ancient World (and the only one whose existence remains unproven) may be inaccurately named. No archaeological evidence of the famed Hanging Gardens of Babylon has been found at Babylon's modern-day excavation site of al-Hillah, but remnants of expansive gardens and advanced irrigation have been unearthed at Nineveh. Also, Babylonian gardens are not mentioned in any contemporary Babylonian textual sources; Sennacherib's annals, however, do describe Nineveh's gardens and irrigation system. Based on the archaeology and analysis of Sennacherib's inscriptions, today most Assyriologists believe that the gardens were at Nineveh when the city was captured by the Neo-Babylonians.[6]

The gardens were first described by classical historians, including Josephus, who had no primary sources on which they based their assertions and only loose understandings of Mesopotamian history informed by hearsay. As we will learn in the next chapter, the Neo-Babylonian Empire had an outsized impact on history considering its short existence of only eighty-seven years. The *renown* of the Neo-Babylonians may have overshadowed the *reality* of seventh-century Mesopotamian life, leading classical historians to conflate Babylon's achievements with those of their Neo-Assyrian predecessors. Only the work of archaeologists could bring to light the inaccuracies and show modern readers how the ancient world truly looked when Jonah was called to prophesy to the Neo-Assyrians.

## A Different Kind of Literature

The book of Jonah has a rich historical setting made tangible by artifacts and structures still being uncovered in Iraq and preserved in museums around the world, but notice that most of the historical details are missing from the Scripture itself. This is because Jonah is not classified as a historical book but as a prophetic one. Yet even as a piece of prophetic literature, Jonah stands alone. Unlike the other prophets such as Isaiah and Jeremiah, the book of Jonah is almost entirely narrative with an unknown author. The actual prophecy is limited to just five Hebrew words, translated as "Forty more days, and Nineveh will be overthrown!" (Jon. 3:4 NASB), whereas other prophetic books are almost entirely prophecies with very little narrative story.

Jonah is unique in format, tone, and purpose, which may be why it is so popular for children to study. It is then surprising that as adults we tend to ignore the entertaining aspects of Jonah simply because it is a book in the Bible. We think that because it is bound in leather, has gold-edged pages, and has been translated in the same tone as Leviticus and Lamentations, then it must be serious. It would feel irreverent and uncomfortable to laugh along with Scripture, so we adults typically refuse to do so.

The problem with that austere view of Jonah is that the story is styled as a farce, a literary genre that uses exaggerated and improbable situations to teach truth through obvious comedy. As literature, the book of Jonah has more in common with *Don Quixote* than with the historical Samuel–Kings or the prophetic Isaiah.

When I was my young cousin Matt's age, learning about Jonah and the "whale" on Sunday school flannel boards, I pictured him bobbing around inside the creature's stomach the way Geppetto sailed inside Monstro before getting sneezed out in Disney's

*Pinocchio*. My generation was taught Jonah as a cautionary tale: Obey God's commands or you'll get to hang out with rotting fish carcasses inside a whale belly. That moral of the story isn't technically wrong, but it also isn't the point of the book. Jonah is not a biography of a bad prophet; it is a farcical tale of a man who thinks he is more deserving of God's grace than his enemies are. We are supposed to identify his actions as absurd because everything that happens in the book is extreme:

- God says, "Travel about 500 miles east to the city of Nineveh." Instead, Jonah decides to sail about 2,500 miles west to the tip of Spain. That's a different mode of transportation in the opposite direction for five times the distance.
- God sends a hurricane to stop one ship from sailing the Mediterranean. Jonah says, "Drown me and the winds will stop." He hits the water and there is instant calm.
- A fish carries Jonah back to dry land. A fish.
- God says, "Go give My message to the people in Nineveh." Jonah takes about three steps into a city described as being the size of Los Angeles, and he says to no one in particular, "God is going to kill you in forty days." With no instructions on how to prevent that, all of the Ninevites—including their animals—turn from their evil ways in outwardly dramatic fashion.
- Jonah climbs a hill and pouts because God is just too nice to everyone, including Jonah. God refuses to kill Jonah as the prophet requests.
- The salvation of 120,000 people doesn't teach Jonah the value of God's mercy, so God kills a day-old bean plant just in case that might do the trick.

Then we are left hanging: "You have had pity on the plant for which you have not labored, nor made it grow, which came up in a night and perished in a night. And should I not pity Nineveh, that great city, in which are more than one hundred and twenty thousand persons who cannot discern between their right hand and their left—and much livestock?" (4:10–11). God asks Jonah a rhetorical question, but we never hear the answer. We are left to consider the events and answer for ourselves.

## Where Did Jonah Go?

If readers approach the book of Jonah as if it were a history textbook retelling of Jonah's actions, then there are several problems. Chief among them is the setting itself: Nineveh prior to 722 BCE. As we now know, the city of Nineveh was not the imperial capital until long after Jonah's pronouncement. Even at its height twenty years later, it was "only" half a mile in diameter and not the roughly sixty miles ("a three-day journey in extent") described in Jonah 3:3. This has led theologians to ask, could the narrator have mistaken Nimrud for Nineveh (which would fit the chronology but does not address the size issue), or could the narrator have used "Nineveh" as a regional description instead of a proper city name? Nations are often known by the names of their capital cities, as the Northern Kingdom is sometimes called Samaria. If Nineveh is used as shorthand for its region and not just a description of the space within the city walls, then Jonah's description of the city's size makes more sense.

But the answer may be literary and not geographical. Scholars have argued for centuries over when the narrator wrote the book of Jonah. Certain words may or may not have been borrowed from other cultures, leading to estimates between the sixth and fourth centuries BCE. The text itself does not indicate who the narrator was or when he lived, but it does give one easy-to-miss clue: By the time this scribe was working, "Nineveh *was* an exceedingly great city" (3:3). That one word puts the writing after 612 BCE, when the Neo-Babylonians conquered the city and began their three-year campaign that destroyed the Neo-Assyrian Empire.

Because of the Neo-Assyrians' brutality against surrounding nations and Israel itself, the city of Nineveh became a symbol for evil throughout the Hebrew Bible, as did Babylon. Even if the city Jonah entered was Nimrud instead of Nineveh—both of which were significantly smaller than the book describes—the theological point remains the same. God asked His prophet to go to the largest city in the world at that time, which happened to be the very center of paganism and brutality, and for at least a moment, those people repented. For that moment, the Northern Kingdom was saved from its coming destruction by Shalmaneser V.

### What Swallowed Jonah?

Just as some people have become obsessed with finding natural causes for the Egyptian plagues instead of simply accepting them as one-time-only, uniquely crafted miracles of God, Bible readers have long wondered just what kind of "great fish" swallowed Jonah in the Mediterranean. A Google search will turn up apologetics sites arguing over which whales and sharks are large enough to hold a human, how stomach enzymes might affect flesh, and even the story of a Massachusetts lobster diver who claims to have spent thirty seconds inside a humpback whale in 2021.[7] Just as fish are drawn to shiny objects, we humans seem to be more interested in the mysterious details of God's works than the message He has for us in Scripture.

The text tells us that Jonah was thrown into the Mediterranean Sea by the sailors who had been taking him to Tarshish. Most scholars have identified Tarshish with the Phoenician colony of Tartessus in southwestern Spain, but the Bible could be referring to another island in the Mediterranean. (As with the species of the fish, the exact location of Tarshish is less important than the fact that it was in the opposite direction of Nineveh.) Once Jonah was in the sea, we read that "the LORD had prepared a great fish to swallow Jonah. And Jonah was in the belly of the fish three days and three nights" (1:17). Why three days and three nights? Did he need that long to pray and contemplate his choices, or did the fish simply need that long to get him back to shore? These are questions with no exact answers.

While inside his personal submarine, Jonah prayed. The very reluctant prophet, who in the end still won't be a model of obedience, did have a change of heart. Although he seems to have blamed God for his predicament ("You cast me into the deep . . . Your billows and Your waves passed over me" [2:3]), Jonah did recognize that God had saved him in a most unusual way, and he did promise to give a sacrifice of thanksgiving (2:9). Only after Jonah's prayer does God command the fish to "vomit" him onto dry land.

We can't know what swallowed Jonah. It could have been a whale (which ancients likely would have called a fish) from the depths of the Mediterranean, or God could have made a special creature just for this one occasion. No matter the vessel, God saved Jonah from drowning in a way that only He could. And that act of kindness (disgusting though it may have been) motivated Jonah to follow God's instruction and impact the lives of the Ninevites and all who were subject to them.

## What Is the Sign of Jonah?

It has been said that the oldest Christian symbol is the *ichthys,* the so-called Jesus Fish. We find it on Christian tombs beginning in the second century, and it has appeared on the backs of cars since the 1970s. It's a simple design of two intersecting curved lines, often with IΧΘΥΣ (the Greek letters for "fish" and an acrostic for "Jesus Christ, God's Son, Savior") inside the fish's "belly."

Fish are throughout all four gospel accounts because fish were central to life in the Mediterranean world. The Gospel of Matthew records that many of Jesus's followers were fishermen (4:19), Jesus famously fed thousands with fish (14:19), and Peter paid taxes with coins found inside a fish's mouth (17:27). Jesus even made His last appearance at a fish fry (Luke 24:36–53).

For the Jews of Judaea, the most famous fish story was that of the prophet Jonah, which Jesus referenced in Matthew 12:38–40:

> Then some of the scribes and Pharisees answered, saying, "Teacher, we want to see a sign from You."
>
> But He answered and said to them, "An evil and adulterous generation seeks after a sign, and no sign will be given to it except the sign of the prophet Jonah. For as Jonah was three days and three nights in the belly of the great fish, so will the Son of Man be three days and three nights in the heart of the earth."

Early Christians embraced Jesus's reference to Jonah, as it came to represent not just Jonah's deliverance after three days in "the belly of Sheol" (Jon. 2:2) but also Jesus's resurrection after three days in the tomb. Scenes from Jonah's ordeal have been found carved into Roman sarcophagi, cut into gemstones, featured in countless religious artworks, and possibly engraved on an ossuary.[8] However, I'm yet to see such elaborate designs on the back of an automobile!

## Conclusion

If we try to read Jonah's adventure seriously—or literally—then this is the most bizarre story in the history of the world. It is easy to mock Jonah, thinking we know better and behave better than the prophet, but really, we are like the prophet. We, too, want to limit God's grace to only those people whom we think deserve it. We will bend over backward—sail through a hurricane or sleep in the belly of a fish—to see our own enemies punished when we are no better than they are. That is absurd behavior, and God knew it would take an absurd story to show us our own prejudices.

After His death and resurrection, Jesus sent His followers to share the gospel with all nations. Matthew ends his Gospel with that command, popularly known as the Great Commission (28:18–20), while Luke uses it as the jumping-off point for part two of his writings, the Acts of the Apostles. The time for early Christians to live only among themselves was over. There was a great big pagan world surrounding them—and even ruling within Judaea—and Jesus called them to interact with it.

Today we are still called into the world. All the continents are linked by technology and transportation, which means that two thousand years after Jesus's death there is more of the world to reach, but it is easier to access both physically and virtually. And yet, interpersonal relationships are becoming more difficult as we are both connected to and separated from each other by screens. It is difficult to love neighbors we have never met, yet our words—be they kind or cruel—can reach the other side of the world in less than one second.

What if Jonah had done more than just the bare minimum in his mission to the Neo-Assyrians? What if he had taken the time to go into the center of the city and speak to its citizens at length, instead of doing the ancient equivalent of tweeting his warning to the few people who happened to hear his comment? History tells us that the people's repentance did not stick; the ten tribes that made up the Northern Kingdom of Israel were conquered and exiled in 722 BCE. Was it because they never knew Jonah or witnessed how God worked in and through His reluctant prophet? I think these are the questions we are left to consider at the end of the book, alongside God's own: "Should I not pity Nineveh, that great city, in which are more than one hundred and twenty thousand persons who cannot discern between their right hand and their left—and much livestock?" (Jon. 4:11).

As Scripture readers, we need to look well past the big-fish miracle and connect with the prophet. We need to recognize what he did wrong (working against God's plan and hating his neigh-bors) and what he did right (finally following God's command). Being a better disciple of Jesus might mean investing time in the lives of those around us, so that God gives us the opportunity and the burning desire to share what we've learned from Scripture and history with open hearts.

# Israel's Lost Tribes, Temple, and Testimony

**F**ill a room with a dozen multigenerational Tennesseans, and you are likely to get two dozen stories about their families' Native American ancestors. My husband, who grew up within a few miles of President Andrew Jackson's Hermitage home, had a third-great-grandmother who was Cherokee. His family keeps an ancient photograph of her, but all of the family's census records and marriage certificates burned along with the Cannon County courthouse in 1934. One branch of my family similarly believed we had a Cherokee ancestor, and my grandmother was incredibly proud of that heritage.

In the mid-1980s, my grandparents booked a one-night trip to Cherokee, North Carolina, for themselves, their children, and their grandchildren. We stayed in a casual motel with interior doors connecting the rooms and rocking chairs on the covered sidewalk in front of our thresholds, and we bought tickets to watch *Unto These Hills*.

On July 1, 1950, the play debuted in the same outdoor amphitheater where it is still performed every summer. It dramatizes the history of the Eastern Band of Cherokee Indians from the arrival of Europeans through their forced migration along the Trail of Tears to a reservation in modern-day Oklahoma in 1838.[1] When I saw it, most of the actors were Native Americans, although that is not the case today. The script has been rewritten several times since 2000, and attendance has waned.

Under Andrew Jackson, the United States Congress passed the Indian Removal Act of 1830, which allowed the government to forcibly relocate the Cherokee, Muscogee, Seminole, Chickasaw, and Choctaw nations from their native lands in the southeastern states to reservations west of the Mississippi River. The Cherokee were the last to go. In June 1838, the US Army began moving sixteen thousand Cherokee from their homes in Alabama, Georgia, North Carolina, and Tennessee. Over the next nine months, the people traveled by road and water. More than one thousand died along the way, and hundreds deserted.[2] Today, there is no reservation for any Native American tribe in Tennessee, but thirty thousand Native Americans are residents of the state.[3]

In recent years, DNA and genealogical research have taught my family that we have no biological connection to any Native American tribes. As a descendant of English Pilgrims and Scottish whisky smugglers, your red-haired author has more in common with the president who supported the Cherokees' forced migration than the people who were exiled, even though I live near places called Moccasin Bend, Chickamauga, Etowah, and Tellico.

I cannot tell you exactly why my family thought we had Cherokee ancestors or how any family's ancient lore develops. Every individual has many lines of ancestors, but usually the only ones we know about are the famous (in my case, Pilgrims) or infamous (whisky smugglers)! The hardworking farmers and homemakers who migrated for better lives and toiled to build futures for their descendants are too often mere lines on a family tree or faded engravings on a headstone.

I now know quite a bit about my ancestors because in the second half of the twentieth century, genealogy grew into a popular pastime in America. Toward the end of the millennium, as computers and the internet ushered in the Digital Age and made our world much smaller, genealogists were able to find distant family members and compare notes and artifacts from their common ancestors. In 2004, the popular British television series *Who Do You Think You Are?* helped celebrities trace their roots with the help of "recreational DNA" and spun off similar shows in other countries that still air today. For the last two decades, we've had history, science, and technology working to bring us closer to our forefathers and foremothers as well as to each other.[4]

But genealogical research is not so new within the Jewish community. Throughout the Bible, we see lists of names from all twelve Israelite tribes in various contexts. While those genealogies might not be perfectly historically accurate (as in the places where Kings and Chronicles or Matthew and Luke disagree for theological reasons), they indicate the importance of remembering one's ancestors. For the descendants of the Israelites, who have been conquered and dispersed and murdered by too many other nations throughout history, a family's only connection to their heritage might be the names of their ancestors. In 2017, the Documentation of Jewish Records Worldwide Project was launched to collect every record of every Jew who has ever lived; once finished, the catalog will be available online for free and will virtually connect all who are part of it. Some users may even be able to connect their modern families to their biblical ancestors and the lands allotted to the twelve tribes in Joshua 13–21.[5]

While many of us have lost connections with our family histories due to time, migration, and maybe some indifference, the Native American tribes and the ancient Israelite tribes were forced into their exiles. They were ripped from their homes by conquering foreigners who wanted to subdue the people and utilize their lands. The actors, locations, and dates may have differed, but the results were the same: Tribal identities were entirely lost or fundamentally changed by aggressive empires.

## Ten Lost Tribes

Shortly after King Solomon's death, the United Kingdom of ancient Israel split. Because Solomon had worshiped other gods at the end of his life, God decided to give leadership of ten of the tribes to another man, Jeroboam, who fled to Egypt after Solomon heard the news and tried to murder him (1 Kings 11:26–40). But the people themselves wanted to split for a different reason. King Solomon had required the men to spend their free time building his great cities, and they wanted Solomon's successor and son, Rehoboam, to reduce their hours. Instead, young Rehoboam threatened them with what sounds like slavery: "My father made your yoke heavy, but I will add to your yoke; my father chastised you with whips, but I will chastise you with scourges!" (12:14). But in spite of all the threats, the split was mostly a peaceful one.

### Internal Misbehavior

Jeroboam initially placed the Northern Kingdom's capital at Shechem. Realizing his people might not want to travel to Jerusalem to make their required sacrifices—and fearing his people would change their minds and want to reunite the nation if they regularly mingled with the southern tribes—he built two high places at Dan and Bethel and placed a golden calf at each (12:25–33). In spite of God choosing Jeroboam to rule the Northern Kingdom as a reaction to Solomon's apostasy, Jeroboam immediately doomed his subjects by separating them from Jerusalem, giving them idols to worship, not employing Levites at his high places, and altering Israel's religious calendar.

The fifth king of the Northern Kingdom, Omri, ruled for twelve years beginning around 880 BCE. He moved the nation's capital to Samaria, which made him the "father" of the Northern Kingdom, even though he wasn't its first king. Until its fall to the Neo-Assyrians in 722, the nation would be known as the "house of Omri" (among other monikers), just as the Southern Kingdom was known as the "house of David."

---

### King David at Tel Dan

The boundaries of ancient Israel stretched "from Dan to Beersheba" (2 Sam. 3:10). After the nation split, the Northern Kingdom had two cultic sites: Dan and Bethel (1 Kings 12:29). At Tel Dan, which today sits on the Israel-Lebanon border, archaeologists have found the oldest arched gate in the world (dating to the time of Abraham) and ritual artifacts from around the time of Jeroboam.[6]

Dan's rich cultic history is fascinating, but it might be more famous for its confirmation of the United Israel. In 1993, archaeologists found broken fragments of an Aramaic stele with the first mention of King David outside of the Bible. An Aramean king brags that he destroyed several thousand Israelite and Judahite cavalrymen with the help of his god, Hadad. He then killed their kings. The pieces of the stele do not name any of the men involved in this war, but many scholars associate the stone document with Hazael of Damascus, who defeated both Jehoram of Israel and Ahaziah of Judah (2 Kings 8–9).

The most interesting phrase on the stele is this: "king of the house of David." When Aram encountered the Southern Kingdom, the king didn't call it Judah or Jerusalem or Southern Israel; he called it the house of David. One hundred years after David died, the enemies of the divided kingdom still recognized David as the father of Israel. Mere decades after this stele was created, the Aramean king's brag sheet was destroyed and its fragments were used to build a wall.[7]

---

Ancient Samaria lies nearly eight miles northwest of the modern-day city of Nablus in the West Bank. It was originally excavated by George Reisner and then by Dame Kathleen Kenyon, but they did not publish thorough details of their work. My own adviser, Lawrence Stager, revisited their work and often enjoyed telling us about the palace discovered there. It was a *bit hilani* style, which means "house with windows." It would have had a porticoed entrance hall built with a stairway approach flanked by columns. From a large window, royalty would look down upon their subjects, maybe like the pope sometimes delivers messages from his study window at the Vatican.

After Omri's death, his son Ahab took the throne. He would rule from Samaria with his infamous Sidonian wife, Jezebel, for twenty-two years. Jezebel survived ten years longer than Ahab, ruling as a queen regent with her sons Ahaziah and then Jehoram. In 2 Kings 9, God anointed another man—Jehu—as the next king of the Northern Kingdom. In verse 30, Jezebel prepared herself to speak to her subjects; she "put on her best make-up and fixed her hair, and she stuck her head out her window" (VOICE). Jezebel walked to that public-facing window in her *bit hilani*–style palace, taunted Jehu, and his servants threw her out of it and onto the ground below, where dogs then ate her flesh.

Jehu did remove worship of Jezebel's gods from the capital city of Samaria, but he kept the high places at Dan and Bethel, probably for the same political reasons Jeroboam built them in the first place. At the end of Jehu's life, God allowed the attrition of the Northern Kingdom: The Aramean king Hazael took territories east of the Jordan River from King Jehoram.

### External Pressures

There was a back-and-forth with Aram during the reigns of Israel's next three kings, culminating in Jehoash recapturing the lost cities and then turning against the Southern Kingdom by tearing down some of Jerusalem's defenses and looting the temple. While all the Israelites were fighting among themselves, Aram was conquered by King Shalmaneser III of the Neo-Assyrians, which he boasted about on his Black Obelisk.[8] The Arameans may have been tough neighbors for the Israelites, but the Neo-Assyrians were a vast, aggressive empire.

In 2 Kings 15, we come to the beginning of the end of the Northern Kingdom. After King Joash there were a series of short-lived, wicked kings until a man named Menachem violently took the throne. He was then attacked by Neo-Assyria's king, Tiglath-Pileser III, whom the Bible calls "Pul," in 737 BCE. To save the Northern Kingdom, Menachem paid a heavy tribute to Neo-Assyria,[9] but the peace did not last. A few years later, Tiglath-Pileser returned, conquered a large portion of the Northern Kingdom, and "took the inhabitants as captives and deported them to Assyria" (15:29 VOICE). Shalmaneser V, the son of Tiglath-Pileser III, would finish the conquest of the Northern Kingdom. He "captured Samaria and carried off the Israelites to exile in Assyria" (17:6 VOICE) in 722, as his father had.[10]

The conquests had two major effects on the Northern Kingdom: The ten tribes of Israel that had made up the north were "lost," and the few Israelites who remained in Samaria intermarried with their new pagan neighbors. Between the two conquests in 737 and 722, the Neo-Assyrians exported most if not all of the politically prominent Israelites from the Northern Kingdom and then imported refugees from other conquered areas of the empire. This was a common practice for ancient conquerors; a mixed population weakened the defeated nation and made future rebellion against the empire less likely.

There are a lot of traditions and theories about the so-called lost tribes. What Scripture says, and what history corroborates, is that the people of the Northern Kingdom were removed from their God-given territories. They were dispersed, not as a group but as individuals, throughout a vast, diverse empire because the Neo-Assyrians wanted the ten tribes' descendants to lose touch with their cultural heritage. And faced with the coming invasion, some people fled—it seems that Jerusalem had an influx of immigration that required Hezekiah to improve the Southern Kingdom's infrastructure.

## Two(ish) Remaining Tribes

While the Northern Kingdom was struggling against the Neo-Assyrians, a new Judahite was anointed king over the Southern Kingdom's tribes of Judah and Benjamin (and the Levites who served at the temple). Hezekiah would face some of the same difficulties his Northern neighbors had.

From the beginning of 2 Kings 18, we are told that Hezekiah "did what was right in the sight of the LORD, according to all that his father David had done" (v. 3). His story begins with a summary that emphasizes the religious reforms he made in the Southern Kingdom. He destroyed any object that could be worshiped—from Asherah poles to a bronze serpent that had been made by Moses—and enjoyed God's favor. I think we are meant to notice that his goodness and greatness come from his devotion to God and not his personal achievements. In 2 Chronicles 29–31, we read about Hezekiah's religious reforms that surely kept the Southern Kingdom from being conquered at the same time the North was. He repaired the temple, which had been closed during the idolatrous reign of his father, Ahaz, and instructed the Levites to cleanse it and themselves so proper worship of God could resume. He then hosted a massive sacrifice to God and invited all the people—from Dan to Beersheba—to bring their sacrifices to the newly reopened temple. Hezekiah didn't cleanse the temple just for the Southern Kingdom but for all Israelites.

Following the restoration of worship at Jerusalem's temple, the people returned to their homes. Wherever they went, they "threw down the high places and the altars" (31:1). We see evidence of this at several archaeological sites. At Tel Beersheba, a four-horned altar was discovered; its horns had been knocked off in an act of desecration before parts of it were reused to build a later wall. At

Tel Arad, there was a complete temple that was in use at the same time as Jerusalem's temple, but it fell out of use around the time of Hezekiah's reign. And at Tel Lachish, an entire temple with two four-horned altars was found inside the city gate; the horns had been knocked off the altars, and the site was further desecrated by having a toilet installed over it—because nothing is more unclean than that! Hezekiah's restoration of the temple seems to have inspired his people to do the same in their own cities.

### Thwarted Neo-Assyrian Assault

Unfortunately, these religious reforms were not enough to permanently save the Southern Kingdom. In 2 Kings 18, after a summary of Hezekiah's religious reforms, we read that Neo-Assyrian king Sennacherib V attacked all of Judah's fortified cities including Lachish. Lachish was the second-most-important city in the Southern Kingdom because of its proximity to Jerusalem. Lachish was well fortified with a six-chambered gate, three-meter-thick walls, a glacis, and a moat. The Neo-Assyrians used stone and dirt to build an earthen rampart 70 meters wide and 16 meters tall so their siege machines could reach the walls and force them down with battering rams. The siege ramp is still there today; it is the oldest in the world and the only known Neo-Assyrian ramp.

The siege of this city is detailed in the Nineveh reliefs on view today at the British Museum. In them, Sennacherib recorded that he took forty-six cities and besieged Jerusalem until it became a vassal.[11] The biblical version confirms Sennacherib's account, although it gives a lower figure for the amount of tribute Hezekiah agreed to pay (18:14–16). Hezekiah apparently stripped all of the gold and silver from his treasury and the newly restored temple to meet the high price, but the Neo-Assyrians still left their outpost at conquered Lachish and marched on Jerusalem.

While he was unable to stop Sennacherib's capture of the walled cities outside the capital, Hezekiah did take effective steps to stave off the Neo-Assyrian assault against Jerusalem that would be helpful in future attacks. Hezekiah's building projects are mentioned across 2 Kings, Isaiah, and 2 Chronicles. He fortified Jerusalem's walls, but most famously, he figured out how to keep access to fresh water for his population during a siege. In order to provide Jerusalem underground access to the waters of the Gihon Spring, which lay outside the city, he "dammed the water sources" (2 Chron. 32:3–4) and ordered a subterranean channel 533 meters long to be chiseled out of solid stone. Hezekiah's Tunnel still holds clean, cold, running water today.

Hezekiah showed his wisdom in the fortifications he prepared for Jerusalem, but at the end of his life, he made one very poor decision. When visited by a prince of Babylon, he gave the man a tour of his palace, treasury, and all the surrounding areas (2 Kings 20:12–19). Maybe it was an unwitting error by a sick king attempting to be diplomatic, or maybe it was a rare show of hubris—regardless of the reason, Hezekiah gave a future enemy a reason to attack Jerusalem.

### Successful Neo-Babylonian Conquest

After the Neo-Assyrians took most of the Southern Kingdom, Hezekiah died and was followed by a notoriously wicked king, Manasseh, who reigned for fifty-five years; his son, Amon, who ruled for only two; and then another reformer, Josiah, who would rule for thirty-one years.

Josiah came to his throne at the age of eight, after his predecessor was murdered by courtiers. Chronicles tells us that he began to follow God at the age of sixteen and to clear out illegal cultic practices by age twenty. His most famous act for the nation—mentioned in both Kings and Chronicles—came when he was twenty-six years old. Josiah orchestrated another renovation and restoration of the temple, and there the workers found the "Book of the Law"—which would have been scrolls, as books were yet to be invented—around the year 628 BCE (2 Chron. 34:14). We don't know exactly what these scrolls contained; they may have been one of the many books mentioned throughout Kings and Chronicles that have not been found, but most theologians and scholars assume it was an early version of the book of Deuteronomy.

As Josiah was making his reforms and doing his best to return his people to right worship of God, the Neo-Assyrians' power was waning due to internal revolts. According to the "Chronicle Concerning the Early Years of Nabopolassar" tablet,[12] in 627 BCE a new generation of leaders in Babylon challenged their Neo-Assyrian leaders, warred, and brokered peace. It was clear that Neo-Babylonia was on the rise, and Neo-Assyria turned to her old enemy and current vassal—Egypt—for military support. In 609, Pharaoh Necho II marched north, necessarily crossing the Southern Kingdom to get to the Euphrates River and help Neo-Assyria. Josiah heard of this, and he took his army to meet Necho at Megiddo. There, Josiah was shot with an arrow and died once he reached Jerusalem (2 Chron. 35:20–24). Necho turned the Southern Kingdom into a vassal state that was forced to pay a heavy annual tribute to Egypt.

In 605, Pharaoh Necho and the now-infamous Neo-Babylonian warrior and king, Nebuchadnezzar II, met at the Battle of Carchemish, where Egypt lost badly. The army was pushed back to the African continent, and all their vassals in the Levant went to Neo-Babylonia. In 598, Nebuchadnezzar returned to the region, exiled the Egypt-backed leaders, plundered Jerusalem, and appointed Zedekiah as the king of the now-Babylonian vassal state.

Zedekiah reigned for eleven years before Nebuchadnezzar slaughtered everyone "without regard to gender, age, or health. They plundered every treasure in the Eternal God's temple and burned God's temple to the ground. They stole the king's and the officers' possessions, tore down the wall of Jerusalem, burned the fortified buildings, and destroyed anything of value in Jerusalem. Anyone who managed to survive the invasion was exiled to Babylon, where they remained servants of the Babylonian court until it was conquered by the Persian Empire" (2 Chron. 36:17–20

VOICE). The version in 2 Kings is slightly different, as the commander "spared the poorest people and left them to take care of the land as farmers and gardeners" (25:12 VOICE). These actions in 586 BCE are reminiscent of the Neo-Assyrian conquest model, in which the important residents were exiled while the weak residents were allowed to stay. One big difference is that Neo-Babylonia did not import exiles from other nations to Jerusalem—possibly because the city was leveled and could not support a larger population.

In 586 BCE, the Southern Kingdom was only Jerusalem and its environs. The people who called it home were members of the tribes of Judah, Benjamin, and Levi—although members of other tribes may have migrated there from the north after 722. These three tribes are not considered to be "lost" in the same way that the northern tribes were.

Today, as DNA testing is showing us some of our ancient roots, specific markers for the twelve tribes have not been identified. However, that may be changing! In 2018, at the Jerusalem-adjacent site of Kirjath Jearim—where the ark rested for twenty years before King David had it brought to Jerusalem (1 Sam. 7:1–2; 2 Sam. 6)—archaeologists discovered a family tomb that had been used from 750 to 650 BCE that contained just enough DNA material from two individuals' petrous bones for testing. More samples are needed in order for the discovery to be practically useful, but for now scientists have learned that this particular Israelite family had ancestral ties to the Canaanites, who themselves came from Anatolia and Arabia.[13]

## Who Were the First Jews?

Once Jerusalem was destroyed in 586 BCE, Nebuchadnezzar II followed the evil empire playbook and exiled all of Judah's leaders to Neo-Babylonia. Whereas Neo-Assyria had removed all of the Northern Kingdom's citizens from their homeland and demanded assimilation,

Nebuchadnezzar left some people in Judah and allowed those who were exiled to continue worshiping their God. For seventy years, the exiled southerners and their homebound relatives retained their religious and national identities as best they could without the temple or self-governance.

While in exile, the southerners, who were mostly Judahites but also Benjaminites and Levites, had their national name shortened. They became known as "Jews" for the first time while in Babylonia. Once Persia conquered Neo-Babylonia, the Jews returned home and rebuilt their nation. When Alexander the Great then conquered the Persian Empire, the name of the Jews' homeland became Hellenized—that is, influenced by the Greek language. The pronunciation and spelling changed from *Judah* to *Judaea*, as that region is still called by Israelis today.

So when you are talking about God's people in the Hebrew Bible, remember that they aren't *Israelites* until after Jacob's name is changed, and they aren't *Jews* until after the Southern Kingdom is exiled.

---

## Where Is the Ark of the Covenant?

This is the question I'm most often asked when people find out what I do for a living! I'll spoil this section and answer it now: No one knows. The ark has not been found by any archaeologists—real, fictional, or pseudo—and there is no mention in the Hebrew Bible of its theft, destruction, or rescue. The ark is last seen as it is placed inside the first temple after Josiah's rediscovery of the law and restoration of Israel's religion (2 Chron. 35:3). God then mentions it in Jeremiah 3:16 in the negative: "They will say no more, 'The ark of the covenant of the LORD.' It shall not come to mind, nor shall they remember it, nor shall they visit it, nor shall it be made anymore." By that time, however, it may have already disappeared.

The Bible gives us a thorough description of the ark, but let's start with the name itself. The Hebrew word our English translations render as *ark* comes from a root that means "to gather." At its most basic, an ark is simply a box made to hold the objects that have been placed inside it. In the case of Noah's ark, the boat-box "gathered" the remnant of life God chose to save from the flood. Other kinds of arks include ossuaries (stone boxes that hold the bones of the dead) and chests (donation boxes that hold money). The most famous is God's ark, which gathered the stone tablets of His testimony, which we call the Ten Commandments.

What we usually call the ark of the covenant is more accurately translated as "ark of the testimony" (Exod. 25:10–22). It was made of wood from the *shittah* tree and then completely covered in gold. Gold rings on each of the four corners held gilt *shittah* poles that could be removed but were supposed to stay in place at all times. On the lid was a golden sculpture of two cherubim who faced each other and whose spread wings overshadowed the "mercy seat" that acted as God's throne on the earth.

God gave the specifications for His ark to Moses while he was on Mount Sinai and while the Israelites were in the valley making the golden calf. As the people were wandering in the wilderness and waiting to conquer Canaan, the ark was mobile. The poles were to be rested on the shoulders of the descendants of Levi's son Kohath (Num. 4:15), but even they could not touch the ark itself. As God's earthly throne, it was perfectly pure; the touch of an imperfect human would result in death because purity and impurity cannot coexist (2 Sam. 6:6–7).

For the next seven hundred years, wherever the ark went, so did the presence of God. When the ark was captured by the Philistines, their cities were afflicted with something like the bubonic plague. Whether it rested inside Moses's tent of meeting, at a sanctuary in Shiloh, or later at its permanent home inside the temple's Holy of Holies, the ark gave worshipers access to God. From there, He accepted the offerings and sacrifices that His people gave as acts of worship and repentance. The ark was not a weapon of war but more like a royal standard reminding friends and foes alike that God was with His people.

According to the books of Kings and Chronicles, the first temple in Jerusalem was attacked at least three times by foreign armies before being flattened by the Neo-Babylonian king Nebuchadnezzar in 586 BCE. The Bible doesn't tell us when or how the ark went missing, but a deuterocanonical text that is accepted by Catholics as Scripture and is traditionally attributed to Ezra records a lamentation over the temple's and people's fate: "You see how our sanctuary has been laid waste, our altar thrown down, our temple destroyed; our harp has been laid low, our song has been silenced, and our rejoicing has been ended; the light of our lampstand has been put out, *the ark of our covenant has been plundered*, our holy things have been polluted, and the name by which we are called has been almost profaned" (2 Esdras 10:21–22 NRSV). If this lament reflects historical accuracy, then Ezra envisions the ark being taken by the Neo-Babylonians as a spoil of war.

In another deuterocanonical text, it was concealed in a cave on Mount Nebo prior to 586:

> One finds in the records that the prophet Jeremiah . . . having received an oracle, ordered that the tent and the ark should follow with him, and that he went out to the mountain where Moses had gone up and had seen the inheritance of God. Jeremiah came and found a cave-dwelling, and he brought there the tent and the ark and the altar of incense; then he sealed up the entrance. Some of those who followed him came up intending to mark the way, but could not find it. When Jeremiah learned of it, he rebuked them and declared: "The place shall remain unknown until God gathers his people together again and shows his mercy. Then the Lord will disclose these things, and the glory of the Lord and the cloud will appear, as they were shown in the case of Moses, and as Solomon asked that the place should be specially consecrated." (2 Macc. 2:1, 4–8 NRSV)

Naturally, early pilgrims, explorers, and archaeologists searched every inch of Mount Nebo and the surrounding rises of the Abarim mountain range in Jordan. God showed Moses the promised land from the Siyagha peak before his death (Deut. 34:1–6), and visitors can still see across the Jordan River all the way to Jericho. The Franciscan Order of the Catholic Church bought the property in 1933, but excavations have only uncovered a fourth-century church.[14] No evidence of the ark or of Moses's burial have been located there or in the surrounding peaks and valleys. The nearby site of Khirbat al-Mukhayyat, also called the town of Nebo, did have a walled city during the Iron Age that is currently being excavated,[15] but no evidence of Jeremiah or Moses has been found so far.

Readers of 2 Maccabees should not be surprised that the ark is still missing, as Jeremiah himself explained that it would not be found "until God gathers his people together again and shows his mercy." Even that explanation is cryptic: Who are "his people"? If this prophecy was given in relation to the Neo-Babylonian exile, then should the ark not have been found as Ezra and the Jews were returning to Jerusalem?

Christians only get two mentions of the ark in the New Testament, neither of which is particularly helpful for locating it. In Hebrews 9:4, the writer adds "the golden pot that had the manna" and "Aaron's rod that budded" to the contents of the ark. Revelation 11:19 gives John's vision of the ark as it sits in the heavenly temple. The latter reference has led some Christians to believe the ark was taken up at some point, but that is a big assumption based on a glancing mention of the box that could very well have had both physical and ethereal forms.

There is one group of Christians who insist they have the ark. The Ethiopian Orthodox Church, which has forty million adherents worldwide, claims to have the real thing in Aksum. As I mentioned in chapter 7, the fourteenth-century writing *The Glory of Kings* describes how the son of the queen of Sheba and Solomon, Menyelek I, brought the ark to Aksum and left a replica in Jerusalem's temple. Today, the church claims to house the ark at

St. Mary of Zion, the 1960s replacement of the sixteenth-century cathedral destroyed by a Muslim army. Only one person on earth knows what is inside that church: the guardian, who is chosen by Aksum's senior priests and "prays constantly by the ark, day and night, burning incense before it and paying tribute to God. Only he can see it; all others are forbidden to lay eyes on it or even go close to it."[16]

For the Aksum tradition to be true, the biblical writers must have had no idea that the ark inside the temple was a fake. All Jewish traditions about the ark's location—including the Scriptures that state it resided in the temple long after ancient Israel split—must be incorrect, and the men who moved the ark must have somehow been descended from Levi's son Kohath. I think it is unlikely that the ark is in Ethiopia today, just as it is unlikely that the Knights Templar moved it to England[17] or that Dr. Jones secured it in the US Army's Hangar 51!

## Conclusion

The ancient Israelites lost their ancestral lands, their family homes, their religious communities, and their God's temple. Everything that had distinguished these tribes from their neighbors was stripped away, except for the memories of peace, prosperity, and self-governance. This leads us to ask, what happens to our personal testimonies when all we have ever known vanishes?

As the Judahites (and Benjaminites and some of the Levites) were sitting in exile and being called Jews for the first time by the very people who had conquered them, they lamented and considered how they had gotten themselves in that situation. They realized they and their ancestors had not worshiped only God in the ways that He required in His testimony of ten commandments. The story of ancient Israel had been one of continual apostasy and then return, sinning and then repenting, punishment and then restoration. So in 539 BCE, when the Jews were given the opportunity to return to Jerusalem and begin again, their leaders, Ezra and Nehemiah, focused on religious purity.

Without a physical temple in which to worship, the exiled Jews turned to their memories and traditions. After the exile, Jewish literature—including the final books of the Hebrew Bible and the earliest midrash—proliferated, and Jewish traditions were instituted. Now-popular holidays such as Hanukkah and Purim developed for the first time, while common symbols such as the Star of David and mezuzah cases were still fifteen hundred years in the future.

The exile was a punishment for God's people, but it also laid the foundation for the Jewish faith as we know it today. It necessarily changed the Israelite religion from being focused on one city and one temple to a faith centered on Scripture, tradition, and community. Although Jews long for the restoration of their physical temple in Jerusalem, they have learned how to take their God with them in rituals and memory, which may be why this tiny religion that first developed at the crossroads of empires during only one century of unity has survived persecution, displacement, and raw hatred for more than three millennia.

# The Jews' Not-So-Silent Years

I am a proud public-school kid. My mother spent her career teaching French and English literature to teenagers, so by the time I reached high school myself, I had an advantage and knew which classes I wanted to take from which teachers. Overall, I had a great education. I was able to enter college with a scholarship and enough credits to graduate a semester early. I was never the smartest student in class—especially not in calculus!—but I may have worked the hardest.

If there was a gaping hole in my secondary education, it was in history. Most of the social sciences were taught by coaches who would have agreed that they merely warmed their rolling chairs between 8:00 a.m. and 3:00 p.m. each day while strategizing warm-ups, workouts, and game plans for their athletes. Within a week of entering college, I realized just how big that hole was. I overheard my private-school-educated dorm mates comparing notes on their high school careers. All seemed to agree that Western Civilization was the hardest secondary class they ever took. "Western Civ," as they called it—a course I had never even heard of—began with the rise of Alexander the Great and explored how Hellenization shaped early European nations, which then spread the ideals of democracy and later Christianity to their non-European colonies, including the Americas. Because I had taken Latin in high school, I had learned the history of ancient Rome and a bit about ancient Greece, but everything else they discussed was unknown to me.

Maybe that particular gap in my public-school education could have been filled by the church, but in many Protestant traditions, the years between the Old and New Testaments are called the Four Hundred Years of Silence. As far as I knew, all people in the world were sitting on their hands between the writings of the prophet Malachi (c. 450 BCE) and the birth of Jesus (c. 4 BCE). But as we are about to learn, those four hundred years were among the most tumultuous in the history of any civilization, Western or otherwise. They changed the map of the world. They were the setting for the arrival of the Messiah, who was born into a Jewish family and nation that was governed by a pagan Roman Empire.

## Building a New Jerusalem

At the end of 2 Kings, Judah's last king, Zedekiah, had watched his sons be murdered, had his eyes gouged out, and was sitting in chains in Babylon. His predecessor, Jehoiachin, was enjoying a comfortable exile eating at the king's table and spending a Babylonian allowance. The Jews themselves did not yet know they would be legally required to live in Babylon for about forty-eight years.

In Neo-Babylonia, the Jews lived in a fertile, comfortable area, and some were able to become wealthy. From Babylonian records, we learn that some Jewish craftsmen were contracted to build projects for Nebuchadnezzar himself. In the later Persian Archive of Murashu, we read about Jews still living in Mesopotamia a century later who were bankers, tax collectors, and superintendents, as well as farmers and fishermen.[1] So while the exile was certainly traumatizing—no people want to be ripped from their homeland after watching neighbors die of starvation during a siege or be murdered by soldiers—the Jews adapted, survived, and remembered their God.

Chronicles, however, describes the events surrounding the exile differently: Nebuchadnezzar's conquest is summarized in just a few verses, Jeremiah's prophecy that the exile would last for seventy years is included (29:10), the conquest of the Neo-Babylonian Empire by the Persians is skipped, and the book ends with Cyrus the Great's proclamation that he would rebuild the temple and permit all the Jews to return to it (36:22–23). The book of Ezra then picks up with exactly the same proclamation. So I have two questions: Why do Kings and Chronicles end so differently, and why does Ezra seem to copy Cyrus's proclamation?

### Why We Need Chronicles

In a Protestant tradition, where Chronicles immediately follows Kings and is categorized as a historical book of the Bible, I grew up being told it was either a flawed retelling of Samuel and Kings or that it was actually one of the books "of the chronicles of the kings" that are often mentioned as sources in Kings. These deep misunderstandings of the text don't stop in children's Sunday schools. Christian translations do casual Bible readers a disservice with their placement of Chronicles because it promotes these incorrect assumptions.

Chronicles is not historical but wisdom literature, as the Hebrew Bible classifies it. Yes, it contains many of the same stories we read in Samuel and Kings, but the writer of those books had a different purpose. Chronicles was written by an unnamed author, whom scholars call "the Chronicler," so that the exiled Jews would remember what was great (and a bit of what was terrible) about their peoples' pasts as they rebuilt Jerusalem and their society. The Chronicler wanted his readers to be inspired by the perfection of ancient Israel under David and Solomon—which is probably why he leaves out most of the negatives, such as Absalom's rebellion and Uriah's murder.

159

Jewish tradition assumes that Ezra is the Chronicler, but that is widely debated. Someone like Ezra—from a priestly family, highly educated, with a practical interest in seeing the revival of Jerusalem—was the writer. But we don't even know that Ezra wrote the book of Ezra. Portions of it seem to be his memoirs, but there are other sections written with a different tone that indicate the book is a compilation. Because of the obvious continuity between Chronicles, Ezra, and even Nehemiah, a common editor seems to have been involved in all.

Chronicles concludes the entire Jewish canon because it is one of the latest books, likely completed in the 400s BCE, and because it is a reflection on the entire contents of the Hebrew Bible, ending on a hopeful note for readers wanting to learn from their ancestors and worship God properly. The Chronicler, as well as Ezra and Nehemiah, wanted their people not to make the same mistakes as their ancestors, whose actions had caused the exile.

### From Neo-Babylonian Conquerors to Persian Benefactors

The Neo-Babylonian Empire had power within Mesopotamia and the Levant for only eighty-seven years, from 626 to 539 BCE. That is less time than ancient Israel existed as a united monarchy under Saul, David, and Solomon!

Cyrus the Great was the founder of the Achaemenid Empire, which is more popularly (and more pronounceably) called the Persian Empire. He was born around 590 BCE, took the throne in 559, won many campaigns between 550 and 540, and then conquered Neo-Babylonia in 539. Not much is known about his early life, but his military exploits are a part of the Mesopotamian Chronicles, and Herodotus's many writings gave him a legendary reputation that would inspire Alexander the Great.[2]

According to the Cyrus Cylinder,[3] which was the emperor's own version of his conquest of Neo-Babylonia, Cyrus began sowing seeds of discord within the city of Babylon. When he arrived with his army, there was very little resistance from the citizens, who seemed happy to have him. All the people must have been shocked at Cyrus's first decree in Babylon. He went to their statue of Marduk, grasped its hands, and declared that he would respect the local and ethnic practices of his new subjects. He had no interest in destroying and dispersing them, as the Neo-Assyrians and Neo-Babylonians had done before him. This attitude of acceptance extended to the Jews, and his proclamation to them is recorded in 2 Chronicles 36:23 and Ezra 1:2–4. He stated that their God had put him over all the nations and had instructed him to rebuild Jerusalem's temple and allow all Jews to return to Judah if they so wished.

Cyrus made that proclamation around 539 BCE, but it was left to a future emperor to complete it. Cyrus died in 530 and was followed by a less-effective and short-lived son, who was then followed by a likely pretender and a lot of palace intrigue. In 522 Cyrus's distant cousin named Darius killed the pretender, took the throne himself, and then spent a year squashing regional rebellions. Darius's conquest of the Persian Empire is described in the Behistun Inscription, which he commissioned the year he took the throne.[4]

Cyrus's policy of allowing his subjects to worship as they pleased continued under Darius. As part of his massive expansion of the Persian Empire in all directions, Darius the Great conquered Egypt in 519 BCE. He had a habit of improving the lives of his subjects while allowing them autonomy of belief. In Egypt, he supported many religious cults, added onto their temples, and completed a canal linking the Nile River to the Red Sea. Therefore, his support of Jerusalem's refortification and temple, as described in Ezra and Nehemiah, seems to be in line with his character and historic policies in other nations.

### What Happened in New Jerusalem?

Establishing the historical timeline for the rebuilding of Jerusalem's temple and fortifications during the sixth and fifth centuries BCE is a challenge because biblical books seem to disagree on the facts.

When we read Ezra in isolation, we learn that the Jews returned to Judaea in waves. The first wave happened while Cyrus was still alive, under the leadership of a "prince of Judah" named Sheshbazzar (1:8) who oversaw the preparations for the second temple. Sheshbazzar might have acted as what we would call a contractor's estimator today: He oversaw the clearing of the site, determined what resources would be necessary to complete construction, and began work on the pad from which the building would rise. The second wave was under Darius, and 42,360 Jews (plus their servants and animals) followed a governor named Zerubbabel. Construction of the second temple was completed "in the sixth year of the reign of King Darius," which was in 515 BCE, but also "according to the command of Cyrus, Darius, and Artaxerxes" (6:14–15). Artaxerxes I was Darius's grandson who ruled between 464 and 424 BCE, when Ezra himself traveled to Jerusalem (7:7).

The inclusion of Artaxerxes I in Ezra 6:14 is likely a result of the Chronicler taking a thirty-thousand-foot view of the events after the fact, but it does throw the timeline into question a bit. Why might he have added Artaxerxes I to the narrative? Because he was the emperor when both Ezra and Nehemiah returned in the third and fourth waves.[5]

It is difficult to separate the works of Ezra and Nehemiah. Even their books are one, called Ezra–Nehemiah, in the early manuscripts. The men had different missions. Ezra, the priest and scribe, was in Jerusalem to return the temple furnishings that had been plundered by Nebuchadnezzar and to use donated funds to establish right teachings and right worship at the new temple. Nehemiah, the cupbearer (that is, close political adviser) to Artaxerxes I, went to Jerusalem to rebuild its infrastructure and fortifications.

We read in Ezra–Nehemiah that the rebuilding effort was not a smooth one. Judahites and Samaritans who had stayed in their homes while their neighbors had been exiled resisted the return of the Jews to Jerusalem. At first the locals wanted to join in the rebuilding efforts, but as they were rebuffed by the exiles, the desire to help became a campaign to derail (Ezra 4). The locals sent tattletale letters to their Persian emperor charging that the Jews would cease to pay their tributes once the temple and city were rebuilt, but the prophets Haggai and Zechariah intervened with God's command that the Jews get back to work and finish the second temple. By the time Ezra arrived, the structure was complete, but the people needed religious guidance.

In the first temple, the Holy of Holies was occupied by the ark of the covenant, and the air was filled with God's *Shekinah* glory. When sacrifices were offered, holy fire would consume the gifts. But the second Holy of Holies was practically empty; only a foundation stone marked the spot where the ark of the covenant should rest. The loss of the ark—whether it was hidden in the mountains, spirited away to another country, destroyed by Nebuchadnezzar, or taken up into heaven—meant that the Israelites' religion would have to change. For the first time, Scripture became the center of daily religious life instead of sacrifices.

In Nehemiah 8, Ezra gathered the people at the water gate and read the "Book of the Law of Moses" to the men and women. We don't know exactly what was contained in this scroll, but most assume it was a version of the Torah and possibly a copy of the scroll that Josiah's men found while repairing and cleansing the first temple. Ezra read to the group, and then the Levites mingled with the people to answer their specific questions. This would be emulated again and again, through to present day, as the central event of a synagogue service. Because God was no longer physically present inside His temple, His written Word was elevated in importance for His followers. Once the second temple was also destroyed in 70 CE, those words and the rabbis' conversations about Scripture (called midrash) would begin to develop into the Jewish traditions we recognize today.

The Persian practices of religious tolerance and local development were widely followed by subsequent empires. From 586 BCE on, the descendants of Judah and Benjamin, and the Levites who worked among them, would be rebuilding their city and nation in the shadow of empires. The Jews would often rebel against their rulers—and managed to rule themselves from 142 to 63 BCE—but never again did they enjoy a theocracy, with both a descendant of David on the throne and God's glory inside the temple.

## Alexander's Ambitions

Far away from Persia and Jerusalem in 336 BCE, the king of Macedon was assassinated by one of his bodyguards. Phillip II had conquered the Greek city-states of Athens and Thebes, and he had then formed a coalition of other Greek city-states with himself as the leader. He intended to attack the Persian Empire, but it was his twenty-year-old son, Alexander, who would do so. Within ten years, Alexander's empire reached from Greece to India and included Egypt.

Any discussion of Alexander the Great must begin with his heritage. He might be the most famous Greek of all time, but History 101 reveals that he was actually from Macedon. He was "Greek" in the same way I am "British"—I was not born there, but my distant ancestors were. Genetically you might call me British, but my nationality is American.

So why do we consider both Phillip II and Alexander to be Greek instead of Macedonian? Partially because of their ancestors. Phillip's family traced its lineage back to Argos, while Alexander's mother, Olympias, was from Epirus. More important than their genealogies was their conscious choice to practice Greek culture no matter where they were. Alexander was educated by Aristotle, so he grew up believing that Greek culture was superior and should be spread throughout the world.

### What Is Hellenization?

As we have learned, the Neo-Assyrian and Neo-Babylonian emperors set out to destroy native cultures. Persian emperors supported the local traditions of their subjects, but the Greeks (and soon the Romans) blended their culture into the natives' practices as a way of pushing the people toward Greek language and practices. This blending is called *Hellenization*, a word that comes from the Greek character Hellen, the first son "born" from a stone to Deucalion and Pyrrha after they survived a world-destroying flood sent by their gods.[6]

One place where Hellenization worked well was in Egypt. When Alexander conquered Egypt in 332 BCE, he adopted the title of pharaoh for himself and he conflated his god, Zeus, with the Egyptians' chief deity at that time, Amun. He then claimed to be the son of this hybrid god, called Zeus-Amun. Subsequent pharaohs, called the Ptolemies, continued to claim this divine lineage and push their Egyptian subjects toward Greek and Roman beliefs and priorities.

There were already a large number of Greek immigrants in Egypt in the fourth century BCE, so it was easy for the Ptolemies to build shiny new cities (such as Alexandria) as centers of art and education in the places where Greeks were already living. Greek language and culture prevailed there. Greek became the official language of the nation, and Greeks filled the upper levels of the aristocracy. The native Egyptians did not prosper in the ways that the Greeks did, and there were frequent uprisings that the Ptolemies thwarted.

Hellenization was not reserved for Egypt; it reached all parts of Alexander's empire with varying levels of influence. At the city of Alexandria on the Mediterranean coast was the famous library that Ptolemy II Philadelphus set out to fill with Greek translations of all the important works of literature in the world. It was during this time (c. 285–246 BCE) that the Hebrew Scriptures were translated into the Septuagint.

The Jewish historian Josephus records a legend of Alexander's arrival in Jerusalem. He describes how Alexander entered the city flanked by priests. He went up to the temple, sacrificed to the Jews'

God, and agreed not to take taxes from Judaea during their Sabbatical year, once every seven years.[7] There is no historical evidence to support this story, and other contemporary sources seem to disagree. The Talmud states that Alexander did not go to Jerusalem at all but was greeted by the high priest and his envoy at Antipatris, just inland from modern-day Tel Aviv. The only physical evidence of Alexander's influence in Judaea are the coins he introduced to standardize the monetary system across his empire.[8] Coins would do two things: show the people the face of the man who ruled them, and smooth trade relations that would enrich the empire.

## What Is the Deuterocanon?

Different branches of the Christian church consider different books sacred. Protestants have the smallest Bible, with sixty-six books, and their Old Testament agrees with the Hebrew Bible (although the order is different). Catholics add seven books written between the Old and New Testaments, which they call the Deuterocanon ("second canon") and which Protestants refer to as the Apocrypha ("hidden"). Orthodox Christians read as many as thirteen more books than Catholics do, depending on their region of the world. Why the discrepancies in canons?

In 1546 CE, the Protestant Reformation was spreading across Europe. The Catholic Church responded by holding the Council of Trent, where church leaders reevaluated the arguments of five Christian theologians from the second to fourth centuries and finalized which books should be included in the New Testament. They accepted the New Testament books, which were also accepted by Protestant churches, but they also included Tobit, Judith, Baruch, Sirach, Wisdom, 1–2 Maccabees, and additional chapters of Daniel and Esther that were part of the Septuagint.

While Protestants and Jews do not view the Deuterocanon as authoritative, several of the books (especially the Maccabees) are helpful writings. They have literary and historical value, even for readers who do not consider them divinely inspired.

### How Did Greeks Become Romans?

Alexander ruled his empire for only thirteen years. In 323 BCE, he became sick after a campaign in India and died in Babylon on June 10. Since he was only thirty-three, there was no real plan of succession. His first wife was pregnant with their first and only child when Alexander died, leaving an empty throne.

At Babylon, Ptolemy, Alexander's general who had been leading the troops in Egypt, recommended to a council that the empire be split into satrapies, with one of the generals ruling each region. Egypt went to Ptolemy himself, Antigonus ruled Asia Minor, Cassander took Macedon, and Seleucus reigned over Persia. These satraps (who are also called the Diadochi, "successors") quickly began to war among themselves, and Ptolemy grew the size of his satrapy. After twenty years of struggles, Ptolemy became an independent king of Egypt, naming himself Ptolemy I Soter (which means "savior") and founding the Ptolemaic dynasty there. Cassander was defeated, and his land was won by Antigonus's descendants who controlled the European lands. The Seleucids would eventually rule all of the Asian lands, including Syria-Palestine. By 200 BCE, Alexander's empire was three nations united by Hellenism and a shared history of violence.[9]

During the post-Alexander wars, the Jews seem to have been living their lives as calmly as possible. Their unofficial national leader was the temple's high priest, who dictated how the people would worship and liaised with whichever emperor was claiming their land at that moment. Wars rocked Jerusalem, and the second temple fell into disrepair even as the Seleucids encouraged temple activities and reduced taxation.

Within Jerusalem, the Jews began to have disagreements among themselves regarding religious practices and the growing Hellenization of the city. Fearing these internal conversations were the rumblings of rebellion, Seleucid king Antiochus IV Epiphanes decided to supercharge Jerusalem's Hellenization and make it into a *polis*, complete with a gymnasium built next to the temple for (naked!) athletics. In a special edict, the king forbade the public practice of the Jewish religion—including making offerings in the temple, observing religious holidays, and circumcising sons—on pain of death.[10] Instead, offerings of unclean animals were made to pagan gods inside the temple, and on December 6, 167 BCE, Antiochus IV committed an "abomination of desolation" (Dan. 11:31; 12:11) by installing a pagan altar over the temple's sacrificial altar and reconsecrating the building in honor of Olympian Zeus.[11]

In the face of culture-destroying evil, the Jews came together. A priestly family called the Hasmoneans conquered Jerusalem in 164 BCE, cleansed the temple, and birthed the Jewish holiday of Hanukkah.[12] The family became high priests and kings, ruling Judaea and growing their nation until it was almost as large as the land allocated for the twelve tribes in Numbers 34.

The Hasmoneans were granted autonomy by Antiochus IV's successor in 142 BCE, possibly because the Seleucids were more concerned with what was happening to their west: The Roman Republic had conquered the Greek peninsula and Macedon in 146. Rome would continue to conquer most of the remnants of Alexander's empire, slowly growing from a republic led by a senate to an empire led by a caesar. In 63 BCE, the Roman general Pompey took Jerusalem, bringing the Hasmonean kingdom back under the thumb of foreign rulers. Then in 30 BCE, Octavian famously captured Ptolemaic Egypt by defeating Mark Antony and the final pharaoh, Cleopatra VII, before becoming the first Roman emperor in 27 BCE and taking the name Caesar Augustus.

## Josephus's Origins and Influence

The non-scriptural writings of Josephus can be a huge help in understanding the blended culture and political climate into which Jesus was born and lived. Because Josephus is one of the few extrabiblical sources for the history of the Jews, we might sometimes take his words as "gospel" history, when the man was actually an unreliable narrator.

Between 66 and 73 CE, the Jews revolted in the First Jewish War. Josephus was a member of the Jewish priestly nobility in Galilee, and he commanded the city's forces against Rome. After his troops were quickly defeated by then-general Vespasian, he essentially defected to the Roman side. He told Vespasian that Hebrew prophecies foretold the general would be crowned as emperor of Rome, so Vespasian kept him around as an interpreter and slave. Once Josephus's own "prophecy" came true, the new emperor freed him, made him a Roman citizen, and commissioned him to write about the Jewish Wars, although his descriptions were riddled with propaganda supporting Roman rule in Judaea.[13]

When reading Josephus, we must remember whom he was writing for—his Roman emperor. Many of his accounts seem to spin history so that the Jews look weak or morally corrupt. The best example of his bias might be in his story of Masada. In 66 CE, a group of Jewish rebels fled Jerusalem and captured Herod's winter palace at Masada, overlooking the Dead Sea. More Jews joined them after Rome destroyed the second temple in 70, and in 73, eight thousand Roman troops laid siege. Josephus's story states that all the Jewish men drew lots, selecting ten who would murder the inhabitants. When only those ten were left alive, they drew lots again and chose one to kill the other nine and then himself.

The story is questioned today, mainly because only twenty-eight of Josephus's nine hundred sixty bodies have been found. Other details in Josephus's story are inaccurate, including his description of the site as having only one palace when there are obviously two. It seems that Josephus never visited Masada himself, and his gruesome story is contradicted by physical remains. It did, however, justify Rome's cruel treatment of the Jews, whom Josephus made to look morally bankrupt and worthy of destruction.

When reading Josephus, we might want to treat his words as we do the reporting from modern news outlets. He had an agenda—to support Roman viewpoints—but his accounts are often the only records we have of Judaean history. So take his writings with that grain of salt, remembering he was neither divinely inspired nor politically neutral.

## Conclusion

While I did not set out to give you a crash course in Western civilization from the perspective of the first Jews, I think it is necessary for where we go next. These conquests, revolts, and cultural shifts are the historical setting for Jesus's life and for the struggles of first-century Jews and Christians.

Those living in the Roman province of Judaea were perpetually caught between their religious leaders and their political governors. In 37 BCE, Rome threw their support behind a Hasmonean named Herod, who would personify this struggle between piety and politics, and named him King of Judaea. As a puppet of the Roman Empire who was prone to personal excess and despotic cruelty, Herod built massive palaces for himself but also the synagogue over the Tomb of the Patriarchs and Matriarchs that is still in use today. He began the work of expanding the second temple into a temple complex, doubling the size of the Temple Mount by building retaining walls that still stand today. He changed how Jews worship, but he also ordered the Massacre of the Innocents (Matt. 2:16–18). And he was the last King of Judaea; the province was divided among his three sons upon his death from a painful and disgusting illness in 4 BCE.

This is the world into which Jesus was born: politically tumultuous, religiously fractured, and culturally blended. Those who lived alongside Jesus understood the political climate; those who would read letters from the apostles knew Greek philosophy and Jewish traditions. As twenty-first-century Scripture readers, we have to bridge the gaps created by time, language, and location in order to understand Jesus's parables, miracles, and sacrifice.

Those four hundred years between the testaments were anything but silent.

# Jesus's Miraculous Life and Death

I n December 2001, my soon-to-be fiancé came to my childhood home for a Christmas meal. While I had been away at college, my parents had decorated the house to the nines: white candles in each window, fresh wreaths and garland on the doors, and a modest nativity set spotlighted between two windows. The mantel was topped with my mother's sizable Santa Claus figurine collection, and four stockings, including a new one for David, hung in front of the woodburning fireplace.

After dinner, we sat in the living room to open the presents in our stockings. They were all addressed "from Santa," as they have been since the year I was born. When David looked at his package, he said, "I didn't grow up believing in Santa Claus." My mother—suddenly remembering his grandmother's Amish heritage—rushed to apologize for addressing the tag as she had. She explained that in our house, stockings are "from Santa" and the bigger gifts are addressed normally. It is just a fun tradition we have. No one was offended, and we went on with a nice evening.

Later that night, after David had left and we were tidying the living room, Mama glimpsed her mantel of two dozen Santas. "He must think I'm awful!" I told her that he did not think she was awful, but that we probably would not teach our children to believe in Santa Claus when the time came (which it never did).[1] David worried that if we "lied" about Santa being real, then our children would think we were lying about Jesus being real. That is a worry I often hear from new parents debating how to celebrate Christmas in their own homes.

I think my parents did a great job of instilling both a love of the season and a love of Jesus in me. On Christmas Eve, we would take a drive around my hometown's Main Street and admire the lights and trimmings on the big old homes. Then, back at our more modest house, I would read *The Night Before Christmas* before my father opened the Bible and read Luke 2. I would beg to open just one gift—a request always denied—and then I'd go to bed while my parents brought out the presents and waited on Santa Claus to come eat his peanut butter and banana sandwich. (Why no cookies? Because Santa needed protein, Mama would tell me. In hindsight, that was also her favorite treat!)

My own childhood belief in Santa Claus waned thanks to another holiday. Each year my parents and I would drive up to visit my maternal grandparents for Easter weekend. On Sunday morning we would attend a sunrise service at their church, and then we would return to the farmhouse for a giant meal with all my cousins and aunts and uncles before hunting Easter eggs—which were mostly L'eggs pantyhose containers my grandmother had carefully saved, filled, and hidden. One year when I was about six years old, I had not quite fallen asleep Saturday night when Grandma slipped into my room to leave a basket filled with cellophane grass, chocolate treats, stuffed animals, colored pencils, and puzzle books "from the Easter Bunny." I lay awake that night, working out that if the Easter Bunny was Grandma, then surely the Tooth Fairy and Santa Claus were actually my parents.

Why did such traditions—or, as some Scrooge-like cynics might say, "elaborate lies"—develop? Anthropologists and historians have written countless dissertations on *how* our current Christmas and Easter traditions were harmonized with ancient nature-based cults determined to keep the sun rising, the sky raining, and the fields growing, but *why* have Christians retained them? I wonder if it might be a desire to pass along feelings of awe to the next generation that we adults have lost ourselves.

During my lifetime, society at large and more specifically the church have had a particular interest in the historicity of Jesus. While the early church fathers debated the nature of His divinity, modern theologians have debated His humanity. The Jesus Seminar was launched in 1985 and continued until 2006.[2] Member theologians asked questions such as, Did Jesus exist as a man? Are the Gospel accounts historically accurate or religious fabrications? Should other writings, such as the Gospel of Thomas, be considered sacred recordings of Jesus's words?

While I do appreciate—and often employ—the sort of historical, textual, and linguistic analyses scholars must use to answer such questions, the questions themselves are flawed for one simple reason: From His conception to His resurrection, Jesus's life was miraculous. The problem for scholars and skeptics is that miracles, by nature, do not leave physical evidence for archaeologists to uncover two thousand years later. No one can prove that Mary was a virgin, that Jesus walked on the Sea of Galilee, or that He resurrected after three days in a tomb.

Adult believers simply accept that these miracles happened in history. Apologists might bend over backward trying to demonstrate to nonbelievers how a comet coincided with the star of Bethlehem or an eclipse darkened the sky at Jesus's crucifixion. But all of that reasoning ignores the miraculous because maybe adults think that we are too smart for awe and wonder. Maybe that is why we continue our unique family traditions at Christmas and Easter and encourage our children to take joy in what cannot be physically explained. By expanding our imaginations from a young age, we increase our abilities to believe in unseen, unprovable, and God-given miracles.

## Jesus's Birth

Jesus was on the earth for only thirty-three years, and he lacked worldly wealth and power, so archaeologists have no physical evidence of Him. Because Roman emperors and Rome-appointed governors did have the ability to leave behind documents and coins and buildings that have remained either intact or in ruins for two thousand years, classical archaeologists can teach us about the world in which the nomadic Rabbi worked, including the political, religious, and societal struggles that He frequently addressed in His sermons and parables. But our primary sources of information about Jesus Himself are the Gospel accounts, which give us four different perspectives of His one life, ministry, death, and resurrection.

The Gospel of Mark is the oldest of the four Gospels and is certainly the most basic. It's just the facts about Jesus's life—no fancy words, no apparent agenda. It opens with John the Baptist announcing the beginning of Jesus's ministry, wasting no time on His birth or childhood.

The Gospel of John is the opposite of Mark; it was finished several decades after the other three Gospels and is much more detailed and theological. Jesus's ministry lasts three years for John, and those three years are filled with events unmentioned by the other writers, such as Jesus curing the blind man at the pool of Siloam (John 9) and raising Lazarus of Bethany from the dead (John 11). Jesus's speeches are significantly longer as John remembers them, and the crucifixion timeline is totally different from the other three.

The Gospels of Matthew and Luke seem to have particular audiences in mind. Matthew's perspective is very Jewish.

Beginning with Jesus's genealogy, which goes back to Abraham, the father of God's people, he highlights how Jesus fulfilled the Jews' expectations for a Messiah. Jesus is descended from King David through his adoptive father, Joseph. He became an exile in Egypt when Herod the Great declared the genocide of young boys (2:16), which is reminiscent of Moses and the exodus. Matthew wants none of his Jewish readers to doubt that Jesus is the Jewish Messiah.

Luke knew he would have a different set of readers—that is, non-Jewish followers of Jesus. As a companion to Paul, Luke traveled to churches throughout the Roman Empire. For him, Jesus is not just the Jews' Messiah but everyone's Christ. He traces Jesus's heritage all the way back to Adam to solidify this point, and he is much more concerned with Jesus's treatment of the poor and society's outcasts than he is with Israelite prophecies. He also goes on to record the development of the early church in the Acts of the Apostles.

Just as Chronicles and Kings give us different perspectives on the history of ancient Israel's monarchies, Matthew and Luke record different details about Jesus's birth narrative with slightly different purposes. As an author, I understand the need to edit for space and for your audience. Neither man could include absolutely everything that happened in Jesus's life, and neither desired to write a textbook accounting of that history. Each was writing to convince his audience of Jesus's divinity, and different stories would resonate more strongly with different readers.

Two thousand years after Jesus walked the earth, those books have been canonized in the New Testament and are read by all Christians, often in immediate succession. We don't typically pick and choose our favorites, and sometimes we must wonder at the differences between them. For centuries, pastors and theologians have attempted to harmonize the Gospel accounts, giving us beloved but sometimes confusing traditions that influence how we honor Jesus's birth, life, and resurrection.

## What Is His Name?

Exactly what you call the Son of God may depend on your religious background and place of origin. In the English-speaking West, you likely grew up calling Him Jesus, but people from Messianic traditions may call Him Yeshua or Yeshu or even Joshua. Why the discrepancies? Good old *transliteration*!

Jesus does indeed share a name with Moses's protégé, Joshua the son of Nun. Their mutual first name means "Yahweh is salvation" in Hebrew, and it transliterates from Hebrew into English as *Yehoshua*. But in our Bibles, the name is never directly transliterated between those languages; Greek and Latin are intermediaries. Remember that in Hellenized first-century Judaea, scribes and rabbis were reading the Septuagint translation of the Hebrew Scriptures. Because Greek does not have letters for some Hebrew sounds, many transliterations could not be exact. Hebrew *Yehoshua* became Greek *Iēsous*. When the name was later transliterated from the Greek into the Latin Vulgate, it became *Iesus*, which was then anglicized as *Jesus*.

But the confusion over His name does not stop there. Today, many people think of *Christ* as Jesus's surname, maybe because it is transliterated as proper names are. However, *Christ* is not a personal name but a unique title that means "anointed one." When the New Testament writers were calling Jesus "Christ," they were translating the Hebrew word we anglicize to *Messiah* (which also means "anointed one") into Greek. This would have been obvious to most of their first-century readers, but it is often lost on twenty-first-century English readers because we don't translate the Greek, we only transliterate it.

### Where Did Mary Labor?

Matthew does not waste many words describing Jesus's birth: Mary "brought forth her firstborn Son. And [Joseph] called His name JESUS" (1:25). Luke 2 has the more detailed accounting, where we read about shepherds and angels in the fields, Joseph and Mary being turned away from a Bethlehem "inn," and Jesus snoozing in a manger. It was the foundation of my own Christmas Eve memories and of Linus van Pelt's beloved monologue in *A Charlie Brown Christmas*, and it was the inspiration for St. Francis of Assisi's first nativity pageant.

On December 24, 1223, Francis performed a midnight mass and staged a *tableau vivant* of Jesus's birth inside a cave near Greccio, Italy. With a chill in the air, a local man and woman put on their best Italian clothes to act as Joseph and Mary caring for a ragdoll infant, and Francis brought an ox and donkey to complete the scene. The pageant was popular and became an annual tradition that continues to this day.[3]

Soon artisans were creating miniature nativity sets—complete with Mary and Joseph in Renaissance finery, three "kings" in Saracen robes and crowns, baby Jesus resting in a straw-lined wooden manger, and every pasture animal you can imagine. The scene I grew up assembling every December had brightly colored plastic figurines set inside a wooden barn with Spanish moss "hay" hot-glued everywhere and a tiny lightbulb "star" poking through the roof. This European-inspired scene rested on a blanket of fake snow.

In the thirteenth century, all Western Christians were Catholic and would need to wait another three hundred years to read Scripture in their own languages. They had to rely on their church leaders to tell them about Jesus. St. Francis's goal of helping his people envision Jesus's birth was wildly successful and has continued influencing our own interpretations of Scripture. When we read Luke 2, we may "see" the wise men who are not there, and we imagine Mary giving birth in a barn even though the biblical text disagrees: "And she brought forth her firstborn Son, and wrapped Him in swaddling cloths, and laid Him in a manger, because there was no room for them in the inn" (Luke 2:7). That one verse plus the account of the shepherds and angels out in the fields that follows it give us the basis for our Christmas nativity scenes but not the particulars.

One word in Luke 2:7 gives English speakers the wrong impression of what happened that night: *katalyma*, which can mean "inn." To be more precise but far less elegant in translation, it is best to read "lodging place" where the KJV and most others have "inn" because we cannot be entirely sure of what Luke is describing. Yes, Bethlehem would have had an inn for travelers, and yes, it is reasonable that it was full because every single descendant of King David was visiting that city to complete the nation's census (Luke 2:1–5). But if Luke means *katalyma* in the sense of an inn, then he expects his readers' knowledge of first-century Jewish hospitality and architecture to explain how a No Vacancy sign led to Mary laboring beside a feeding trough.

In Bethlehem and the rest of Judaea, Jews were obligated by their faith to welcome guests no matter the circumstances. Because it was so common that traveling strangers would lodge a night with any family along their route, Luke may not have been describing an inn at all. Mary and Joseph may have gone to a family's home where there may have been no space in the "upper room" of the house. (The same word, *katalyma*, also describes this type of second-floor space, and it is used by Luke in 22:11 to describe the place where Jesus would host the Last Supper.)

In the first century, homes within the city were designed so that the hot and dirty work occurred on the first floor. There the warm animals would spend their nights, the women would cook with hot ovens each day, and the space could be easily cleaned. The upper rooms were reserved for sleeping, dining, and neater activities such as spinning and weaving because breezes made them cooler in the summer and rising body and kitchen heat made them warmer in the winter. So Mary and Joseph did not go out to a barn in the countryside; they just had to stay on the less-comfortable first floor of a house, where the animals and their mangers were kept, where Mary would have been warm during her labor, and where the new family might have had a bit of privacy from the rest of the household living in the upper room.

### Who Visited the Child?

Matthew's major contribution to the birth narrative comes in chapter 2: *magoi* from the East see "His star" and go to Jerusalem to find and worship the King of the Jews. The biblical text doesn't tell us much about these "wise men." It doesn't tell us how many of them were present, where exactly they came from, or how long they traveled.

As so often happens when Scripture is silent on the details of an event, we readers tend to fill in the blanks with ideas and stories that have developed over two thousand years into Christian traditions. We envision three travelers only because they brought three gifts: gold, frankincense, and myrrh. We call them "kings" because third-century church father Tertullian erroneously linked them to kings who honored Solomon in Psalm 72.[4]

Looking instead to the first-century history of the region, there is a good chance that the magoi of Matthew 2 were Zoroastrian priests. Zoroastrianism was the official religion of the Persian lands from roughly the time of Darius the Great's birth (c. 550 BCE) until the Muslims conquered in 661 CE. During the first century, the kingdom stretched from modern-day eastern Turkey to Afghanistan. The leaders of Zoroastrianism were called *magi* in their own language, their lands were geographically east, they studied astronomy intently, and their Persian ancestors had historical contact with the Jewish people during and after the exile.

It is possible that Matthew wrote enough in his Gospel to identify the magoi as Zoroastrian priests to his contemporary readers, but I tend to think he was intentionally vague about their identities. The point of the visit was that the magoi were among the first Gentiles to recognize and honor Jesus as the King of the Jews— whenever and wherever that may have happened.

### When Did This All Happen?

Dating and locating the visit is not possible based on the biblical texts themselves. Matthew tells us the magoi came to Jerusalem "after Jesus was born in Bethlehem of Judea in the days of Herod the king" (2:1). Herod the Great died in 4 BCE, meaning the birth, the visit, and the family's Egyptian exile all happened prior to that date. But how long before 4 BCE? How old was Jesus by the time the magoi reached Him, and how long did the family reside in Egypt?

Luke's account of the birth does not help, as he places Jesus's birth during the census administered by Quirinius in 6 CE. Various solutions have been proposed to harmonize the accounts. Some argue that Matthew described the wrong Herod or that Luke got his Syrian governors confused. As we understand history today, these Gospels cannot be reconciled; so to figure out which gospel "must" be in error, some will then turn away from history and toward science to try to identify the star of Bethlehem as an astronomical body.

Ancient astronomers noted several natural events during the last decade or so of the first century BCE. Halley's Comet was visible in 12 and 11 BCE, and several novae were visible in 5 and 4 BCE. Maybe the most popular interpretation of the "star" is that a planetary conjunction—when two or more planets appear to meet from the perspective on Earth—would have produced the unusually bright light in 7 BCE.[5] The basic problem with all of these theories is that the magoi would have already known exactly what they were witnessing from a scientific perspective. Some of these phenomena would have even been predicted, as we already know that Halley's Comet will appear again on July 28, 2061.

As Matthew describes the star, it did not behave like any known astronomical body. The star stayed in the sky long enough for the magoi to travel west to Jerusalem from far away. It then moved and remained steady as they traveled south to Bethlehem. The star was a one-time-only creation of God that was likely noticed by the magoi for its uniqueness in the heavens. Any old meteor or comet or planet or even nova would have merited study and documentation but not the sort of journey those men made. The star was a miracle of God, not an incidental natural phenomenon.

We must remember that the Scriptures are theological texts. While history and even science can help us to contextualize what Matthew, Luke, and others wrote about Jesus and the first century, those disciplines are limited by what modern scholars have learned. As archaeology continues to unearth structures and documents that tell us more about the classical world, astrophysics is showing us images of the universe that make us question previously accepted theories of heavenly bodies. Nothing in the natural world is settled history or settled science so long as discovery continues, so we must hold lightly to our own conclusions. That same attitude should apply as we read sacred texts, which are designed to build our relationships with God as we marvel at His awe-inspiring creation and works—not make us self-satisfied with our own worldly timelines and conclusions.

### How Many Herods?

Throughout the Gospels and early Christian history, there are many villains with the name Herod. The most famous is the family's patriarch, Herod the Great, who ruled from 47 to 4 BCE, had ten wives, and ordered the Massacre of the Innocents that sent Jesus's family to Egypt. But after that king's death, the frequently duplicated name Herod can make identifying his descendants and following the history difficult.

Three of Herod the Great's marriages factor into the biblical narrative. Mariamne I was a Hasmonean princess (whom he murdered) whose *grand*children were Herod Agrippa I and Herodias. Malthace was the mother of Herod Archelaus and Herod Antipas. Mariamne II was the mother of Herod Phillip.

Herod Archelaus immediately followed his father as ruler of Judaea, Samaria, and Idumaea (Matt. 2:22), while the rest of Herod the Great's lands were split between Herod Phillip and Herod Antipas. Therefore, three Herods simultaneously governed the lands their father had solely controlled.

Herodias initially married her uncle Herod Phillip and had a daughter named Salome. They divorced, and she married Herod Antipas (Phillip's half brother and her uncle). This second marriage was rebuked by John the Baptist, so Herod Antipas had him killed (Matt. 14:1–11). He also presided over part of Jesus's trial (Luke 23:7–11).

Herodias's brother, Herod Agrippa I, executed James the son of Zebedee and imprisoned Peter (Acts 12:1–11) before being killed by a heavenly messenger for allowing others to worship him as a god (12:20–23). His son (and Herod the Great's great-grandson), Herod Agrippa II, was appointed to hear Paul's defense (23:35).

Scripture is not always clear about which Herod is being described, likely because contemporary readers knew who had been in charge in their own recent histories. Thankfully, the exploits of these men and women were detailed by Nicolaus of Damascus and Josephus in their writings, so modern readers can historically contextualize New Testament events.

## Jesus's Ministry

In life we all have pet peeves—others' use (or nonuse) of turn signals, the superiority (or irrelevance) of the Oxford comma, the horrors (or delights) of daylight saving time. In line with my contention that archaeology *contextualizes* but does not *prove* the Bible is my pet peeve: It is impossible to "walk in Jesus's footsteps" on a tour in Israel.

A "Christian" tour of Israel often means seeing church after church, each supposedly the site of a miraculous event—and often down the street from a competing church honoring the exact same event. In Nazareth are two churches honoring Gabriel's annunciation to Mary: one Catholic and one Eastern Orthodox. In Bethlehem, the Church of the Nativity covers the cave where fourth-century Christians believed Jesus was born. St. Peter's Church in Capernaum encloses the ruins of a first-century house that may have belonged to Peter and was converted to an early home church. Most famously, the Church of the Holy Sepulchre in Jerusalem honors the sites of Jesus's crucifixion and entombment.

These buildings, many of which are old enough to be considered archaeological artifacts themselves, frustrate me because they honor traditions that developed hundreds of years after Jesus lived and prevent us from thoroughly excavating the first-century layers of civilization. They are monuments to religion and may promote narratives that do not appear in Scripture and may in fact conflict with biblical accounts.

The closest we can get to "walking where Jesus walked" is around the Sea of Galilee. During the first century, Capernaum was a bustling fishing village along a heavily trafficked trading route and was home to a Roman garrison. That region is frequently the setting of Jesus's activities as described in the Gospels.

- He lived in Capernaum during much of His ministry (Matt. 4:13; Mark 2:1).
- He performed many miracles in Galilee (Matt. 8:5–13; Mark 1:21–28; 2:1–12; Luke 7:1–10; John 4:46–54).
- He addressed paying temple taxes (Matt. 17:24).
- He taught in Capernaum's synagogue (Mark 1:21; Luke 4:31–38).
- He walked on the Sea of Galilee (Matt. 14:22–34; Mark 6:45–53; John 6:16–20).
- And there He selected Simon Peter, Andrew, John, James Zebedee, and Matthew as apostles (Matt. 4:18–22; 9:9–13; Mark 2:13–17; Luke 5:1–11, 27–28).

Just six miles down the road from Capernaum is the ancient city of Magdala, home to the only person all four Gospels name as being present at Jesus's tomb: Mary Magdalene. The city itself does not feature in the Gospels, and that might be why it doesn't have a church obstructing the original city's ruins! The current excavation of Magdala began in 2009, when contractors preparing the foundation for a new building stumbled on the untouched remains of a first-century synagogue.[6]

Archaeologists have discovered that Magdala first became a city around 200 BCE. By the time Mary was born, it had grown into a prosperous fishing village with a distinctly Jewish culture. It boasts the oldest synagogue discovered in Galilee to date, and the frescoed walls and mosaic floors preserved in several buildings survived flooding, conquest, and a major earthquake. Four high-quality groundwater-fed ritual baths further indicate the importance of the Jewish religion to daily life, and the large marketplace testifies to the city's great wealth.

In both of these cities—Capernaum and Magdala—we can feel the breezes coming off the Sea of Galilee, hear how sounds amplify easily over the water, and envision thousands gathering along its shores to listen to Jesus speak. At Magdala, we can imagine Jesus teaching inside that very synagogue filled with pious Jews. This place was the center of His ministry, even though no objects prove that here He fed thousands and walked on water.

## Jesus's Death

In Old Jerusalem, the Jesus-centric sites are impossible to miss. Embedded in walls are tile signs reading *Via Dolorosa* in Arabic, Hebrew, and Latin. Along these streets, modern Christian pilgrims follow the "Way Full of Pain," the same path that eighteenth-century Roman Catholic tradition says Jesus walked from His trial to His crucifixion. The route is about half a mile long, with stops at each of the fourteen Stations of the Cross.

If you go to the first stop at Madrasa El-Omariya (a local elementary boys' school), you'll find maps of the entire route and a small museum. There, tourist groups prepare to walk the route while carrying a heavy wooden cross past signs indicating where Jesus was sentenced, stumbled, encountered His mother, and had His face wiped by Veronica. The last five stations—where Jesus was stripped naked, nailed to the cross, died on the cross, removed from the cross, and buried—are all inside the Church of the Holy Sepulchre.

The Via Dolorosa was first conceived during the fourth century but was popularized by the medieval Crusaders. Over the centuries, as Crusaders and Muslims swapped control of Jerusalem, the route changed. Sites such as the Praetorium, Antonia Fortress, and even the Temple Mount were once along the route but had to be eliminated due to political tensions and later city development.

Even if Jesus's route to the cross could be somehow verified, the elevations would be wrong. A simple walk along Jerusalem's streets reveals old doorways and window wells that were once at street level but are now basement spaces due to the vertical growth of the city. The streets that Jesus would have walked were destroyed by the Romans in 70, only to be rebuilt and destroyed and rebuilt by successive conquerors over the next nearly two thousand years. Jerusalem, you see, is the ultimate tel hiding millennia of civilizations. It cannot be thoroughly excavated without literally undermining the modern city, so we can only look for Jesus's tomb on the surface or in traditionally accepted locations.

### The Traditional Tomb

No trip to Jerusalem would be complete without visiting the Church of the Holy Sepulchre. Completed in the fourth century CE, after Emperor Constantine's mother Helena identified the site as the location of Jesus's three-day burial, this spot boasts the oldest tradition and the certification of six Christian traditions: Roman Catholic, Armenian Apostolic, and Greek, Coptic, Ethiopian, and Syriac Orthodox churches. All six share the responsibilities of maintaining the massive building, which has been damaged and rebuilt several times, but territorial squabbles continue. To this day, one local Muslim family holds the five-hundred-year-old cast-iron key to the church, and a second Muslim family opens and closes the building every day.[7]

It is easy to spend an entire day inside, visiting each denomination's own shrines and admiring artifacts such as the Stone of Unction (where they say Jesus's body was prepared for burial), the Rock of Calvary (on which Jesus was crucified), Jesus's prison cell, and of course, the Holy Sepulchre itself, where Jesus's body lay for three days.

Inside the rotunda of the Church of the Holy Sepulchre sits the Aedicule, a small, domed chapel that was built over the site of the tomb and the Angel's Stone, a fragment of the rock that closed the tomb. Above the Aedicule is a skylight surrounded by a twelve-pointed star representing the twelve apostles Jesus sent into the world. Each Holy Saturday, Orthodox Christians celebrate the Holy Fire Ceremony. Worshipers believe a divine spark comes through that skylight and lights thirty-three candles held by the Greek Orthodox Patriarch of Jerusalem inside the Aedicule; the people in attendance then share the flame among their own candles and carefully take them home.[8]

This church is packed with history, and it honors two thousand years of traditions with tons of gold, silver, jewels, stained glass, tapestries, and incense. The treasure inside is incalculable, but recent renovations to the building had a budget of eleven million dollars. Those renovations gave archaeologists the chance to excavate around the Aedicule, where they found fourth-century coins and evidence of an older building that once stood in the same place.[9] Although there is no physical evidence proving that Jesus's body ever rested behind the Angel's Stone, it is obvious that Christians did indeed believe it to be His tomb when Helena visited.

### The Protestants' Tomb

Just outside the walls of the Old City sits a rival to the Church of the Holy Sepulchre. Based on anecdotal evidence as opposed to a fourth-century tradition, the Garden Tomb is a walled garden inside the heart of the bustling city.

In 1867, a local began clearing the area for farming. He found a cave halfway filled with dirt and bones, which several European Protestants determined to be Jesus's tomb. The land was purchased in 1894 for two thousand pounds by the Garden Tomb Association, a group of Englishmen including the archbishop of Canterbury. The men put up the walls, cleared the land, and planted the beautiful garden that remains there today.

The dubious identification comes from a nearby rockface called Skull Hill, which looked like a man's face until its nose fell off during a 2015 storm and may have been a site for first-century executions along the road to Damascus. The tomb itself is carved out of limestone, and there are places to lay three bodies. Today, archaeologists believe the tomb was actually carved during the Iron Age, when the Israelite and Judahite kings were ruling the Northern and Southern Kingdoms of Israel. Wall carvings indicate it was reused during the Byzantine period, but there is no evidence that it or any other cave in the area was used for first-century burials.

The Garden Tomb is well worth the visit. It probably isn't where Jesus was buried, but it is a wonderful place for quiet reflection and worship without the glittering decorations and loud busyness that fill the Church of the Holy Sepulchre.

### The Skeptics' Tomb

Not quite four miles south of the Garden Tomb is East Talpiot. There, on Thursday, March 27, 1980, a dynamite blast uncovered a tomb that had been carved out of the bedrock. Inside were ten ossuaries, six of which had names scratched into their limestone sides. One of those inscriptions reads "Jesus son of Joseph." The other names were Mary, Mary Mara, Matthew, Jose (Joses), and Judah son of Jesus.[10]

Since the discovery, some have hypothesized that Jesus's body only spent one night in Joseph of Arimathea's tomb. It was placed there quickly but not permanently due to the Sabbath laws, and was then transferred to His family's tomb in Talpiot, leaving Mary Magdalene to tell Peter and John at the original burial site three days later that "they have taken away the Lord out of the tomb, and we do not know where they have laid Him" (John 20:2). Mary's worst fear—that the grave had been robbed—was confirmed by this discovery, they said, so the Gospel writers must have invented Jesus's resurrection to cover up the theft.[11]

Most scholars who addressed the theory cited three major problems with it: The names on the ossuaries were common in first-century Judaea, the family tomb of Jesus would more likely have been in Nazareth, and most importantly, Jesus of Nazareth had no children! While skeptics may use this tomb to argue Jesus was not bodily resurrected, I see only evidence of a first-century family who either chose to name their children in honor of Jesus and His family or who also used the popular names of the day. There's really no good reason to tie this tomb to the holy family.

## Conclusion

So long as we await Jesus's second coming, we will always be looking for evidence of Him even though He "made Himself of no reputation, taking the form of a bondservant, and coming in the likeness of men" (Phil. 2:7). As our Savior, as the Humble One who reconciled humanity to God so long after Adam and Eve separated us, we naturally want a close relationship with Him. We want to be able to walk in His footsteps and touch what He touched—as we might do in honor of deceased friends and family—because those actions would make us feel closer to Him.

God created us for relationship with Him, and that is difficult for us to understand when all of our other relationships and experiences are physical. We can hug those we love. We can share meals around a table and help one another in times of pain and sorrow. We can visit the tombs of those who have died before us.

In those ways, we are used to tangible relationships, not spiritual ones. I think that is why we work so hard to prove to ourselves and others that Jesus was a historical person and also God.

But from His conception, there was nothing "natural" about Jesus. He was miraculous. Everything He did defied convention. A relationship with Him requires faith, and faith cannot be reasoned or manufactured. It cannot be proven or seen. It is a gift of the Holy Spirit (Gal. 5:22) that we cannot control, and let's be honest with ourselves—humans are control freaks! We want to know everything, we always want to be correct, and we want to surround ourselves with people who think as we do.

God wants us to be in awe of Him. He wants us to trust Him with what we cannot see or comprehend, and that is increasingly hard to do in a postmodern world that encourages division, self-reliance, and relative truth—even within the church itself.

# The Church's Growth and Division

In our twenty-three years of marriage, David and I have lived in big cities and suburban towns. We both come from families with rural roots, and among all those settings, we've learned that religious divisions are inevitable. Rural communities may have reputations for being closely knit and like-minded, but people still find ways to differentiate themselves and their opinions. Even the smallest towns—those without chain stores or traffic signals, where farmers share their large equipment every season—will have disagreements among neighbors. Maybe no one is building a temple to Zeus between the Baptists and the Presbyterians, but different church bodies have big feelings about where, when, and how baptisms should be performed or communion offered.

My mother grew up in such a small town, and I loved visiting my grandparents there whenever possible. Grandpa was usually away, working their dairy farm during my earliest years and then driving his eighteen-wheeler during my adolescence, so Grandma and I had a lot of "girl time." She would spoil me with a drugstore shopping spree of jelly shoes, press-on nails, and Barbie-themed coloring books. On our way back to the house, we would stop at the tiny local grocery to eat grilled cheese sandwiches and drink Dr Pepper from a glass bottle.

Between the grocery and the house was a small Protestant church. I knew Grandma's church well—Christmas Eve candle-light and Easter sunrise services were annual delights, and some-times the elders would let my cousins and me light the candles on ordinary Sundays. But prior to this outing I'd never noticed this other building. "Grandma, that church is so much closer to your house. Why don't you go there?"

She was quiet for a bit. Explaining denominations to a seven-year-old—even one who had already declared her unbelief in the Easter Bunny and Santa Claus—was going to take some finesse. Eventually she said, "They don't believe what we believe."

"They don't believe in Jesus?" I asked.

"They do, but they worship Him differently. And they don't think that *we* believe in Jesus." I know now that particular church is a "closed" denomination; only members of that body in good standing with their own leadership may receive communion, and their leaders boldly state that they and their followers will be the only ones in heaven. But back then I was a little bit hurt by the idea that some Christians claim to know more about my salvation and my relationship with God than I do.

Decades later, I see that all Christians believe we know best about the Scriptures. If we did not think our opinions were cor-rect, then we would think differently! What varies from person to person and denomination to denomination is just how much grace and consideration we are prepared to give those with whom we disagree. Certainly there are essentials to the Christian faith—specifically, unwavering acceptance of Jesus's work to reconcile humanity with God. But where we tend to disagree, puff ourselves up, and justify division from (or even loathing of) others comes from our own interpretations and not from God's Word itself.

Doctrinal divisions are nothing new. Although technology has exacerbated our divisions—while simultaneously making us physically and virtually closer than ever—bold differences of opinion about Jesus's life, death, and resurrection began even before the crucifixion.

## First-Century Divisions

Throughout the four Gospels, the Jewish sects of Pharisees and Sadducees frequently questioned Jesus's teachings about the Hebrew Scriptures. For nearly two hundred years, these groups had been at odds with each other over their own interpretations of the scrolls. Jesus gave them more to argue about but also a common "enemy" to unite them on occasion! There is no scholarly agreement on who the Pharisees were, what they believed, or what exactly they did. They seem to have been reformers who wanted the world to change slowly according to God's will. They valued purity, so they didn't interact with the "unwashed masses" very much, but they were politically active and had a reputation for seizing power from whomever they could. We know even less about the Sadducees: They did not believe anyone would ever be resurrected, they preferred free will to fate, they tended to be wealthy, and they were close to Jerusalem's high priest.[1]

Jesus, His disciples, and the Judaean population had watched these groups squabble, enrich themselves, and hold power over others in the name of their interpretations of God's Word. Maybe that sad example was why Jesus had to rebuke His own apostles for arguing about who among them was the greatest (Luke 9:46–50). Before they would become teachers themselves, His followers had to learn from the Teacher that humility is valuable in leadership, not power, position, wealth, fame, or self-aggrandizement. That lesson would be important once He resurrected and His followers were left to interpret and spread His gospel message.

## Paul's Struggles with the Disciples

In the immediate wake of Jesus's trial, crucifixion, and resurrection, the apostles were left a bit rudderless. After Jesus ascended to heaven (Acts 1:9), the eleven remaining apostles and Jesus's family prayed in an upper room. "In those days" (1:15), the group grew to about one hundred twenty, and the apostles decided it was time to find a twelfth disciple to replace Judas Iscariot. Through the ancient practice of drawing lots, which had been used by judges and priests throughout Israelite history to divine God's will, Matthias, a man who "went in and out among us, beginning from the baptism of John to that day when He [Jesus] was taken up from us" was chosen as the new twelfth apostle (1:21–22).

But many Christians question Matthias's status as the twelfth apostle because he was not selected by Jesus and he never appears in the Scriptures again. We wonder, did the other eleven have the right or responsibility to choose? Was the use of lots an act of seeking God's will, or was the result simply the luck of the draw? If Matthias was the "new" twelfth, then why is Paul called an apostle and why do Paul's letters comprise nearly a quarter of the New Testament?

Paul's conversion from Jewish Pharisee to early Christian is the stuff of legends. The Bible explains how, after witnessing—or maybe overseeing—the stoning of the Christian deacon Stephen, Paul "made havoc of the church, entering every house, and dragging off men and women, committing them to prison" (Acts 8:3). On his way to Damascus, "a light shone around him from heaven . . . and he heard a voice" (9:3–4). Blinded for three days, Paul was healed by Ananias, a disciple who at first protested the commission he'd been given by the Lord. "But the Lord said to him, 'Go, for he is a chosen vessel of Mine to bear My name before Gentiles, kings, and the children of Israel. For I will show him how many things he must suffer for My name's sake'" (9:15–16).

194

## What's in a Name?

In the New Testament, many people have two names. For example, Thomas is also Didymus, Tabitha is also Dorcas, and most famously, Saul is also Paul. These individuals had two names not because of conversion experiences or legal name changes, but because it was common for Roman citizens to have both ethnic (in this case Hebrew) and Greek names.

Saul—who was likely named after King Saul, a great ancestor from his own tribe of Benjamin—would have had the Greek name Paulos from an early age because he had Roman citizenship. He would have used both names in his lifetime, depending on where he was preaching and to whom he was speaking or writing. Jesus did not rename "Saul the Sinner" to "Paul the Apostle" on the road to Damascus. That tradition may have developed as a way to associate him with Old Testament heroes such as Abraham and Israel who actually were renamed by God, but it has zero support in Scripture. The explanation lies in history.

---

After Paul's conversion, he began preaching to the people of Damascus. As some Jews accepted Jesus as their Messiah based on Paul's teachings, other Jews set out to murder him. He fled to Jerusalem, where most of Jesus's followers did not believe he had changed. But a Cypriot disciple named Barnabas vouched for him: "So he was with them at Jerusalem, coming in and going out. And he spoke boldly in the name of the Lord Jesus and disputed against the Hellenists, but they attempted to kill him. When the brethren found out, they brought him down to Caesarea and sent him out to [his hometown of] Tarsus" (9:28–29).

Sometime later, Barnabas followed Paul, and the two spent a year with the church in Antioch where "the disciples were first called Christians" (11:26). They stayed in touch with the Judaean believers, carrying donations to them from wealthier Antioch, and on one trip they picked up John Mark, who acted as their assistant.

He apparently traveled with them to many cities, but in Pamphylia, John Mark inexplicably returned to Jerusalem. Maybe he had a personal matter at home; maybe he was unsettled by the spiritual warfare he witnessed in foreign courts—we don't know why he left Paul and Barnabas, but it must have irritated Paul more than Acts 13:13 indicates. When Barnabas suggested that John Mark join them again at a later date, "the contention became so sharp that they parted from one another. And so Barnabas took Mark and sailed to Cyprus; but Paul chose Silas and departed" (15:39–40). Except for glancing mentions in Paul's letters, which indicate the men reconciled, Barnabas's biblical story ends there.

### Judaizers Versus Gentiles

Just before Barnabas and Paul parted ways, the early church had its first doctrinal crisis: Must Gentiles convert to Judaism before becoming Christians? Some Judaeans had been teaching, "Unless you are circumcised according to the custom of Moses, you cannot be saved" (Acts 15:1). Historically speaking, this is a strange position for the Jews to take. With the notable exception of the Hasmonean king and high priest John Hyrcanus I, who grew the boundaries of Judaea and attempted to force Idumaeans to convert to Judaism at the end of the second century BCE,[2] Jews were not proselytes. The Hebrew Scriptures were clearly against the blending of Israelites with their pagan neighbors, and rare are the stories of conversion. Canaanite Rahab and Moabite Ruth—who were ancestors of both David and Jesus—come to mind.

Paul and Barnabas returned to Jerusalem to speak against the idea of converting Gentiles to Judaism. Acts does not record the Jews' reasoning for preaching conversion; we only read Peter's thorough rebuttal of the idea and the council's conclusion that Gentiles should "abstain from things offered to idols, from blood, from things strangled, and from sexual immorality" (15:29).

Note Paul's possibly unexpected position in this argument. As a Pharisee, Paul had a deep knowledge of the Hebrew Scriptures.

He knew Jewish traditions and rituals better than anyone, and we might expect that as a "fundamentalist" Jew he would be on the side of his fellow "Pharisees who believed [in Jesus]" (15:5), but he was not. Paul and Barnabas described the miracles and conversions they had witnessed during their travels among the Gentiles, and they agreed with Peter that "God, who knows the heart, acknowledged them [the Gentiles] by giving them the Holy Spirit, just as He did to us, and made no distinction between us and them, purifying their hearts by faith" (15:8–9). Peter's position seems not to have been a natural one for him either—in Galatians 2:11–21, Paul recounts his confrontation with Peter over exactly this issue.

The Gentiles rejoiced at this decision (Acts 15:31), but the matter was not completely settled. Three hundred years later, the Council of Laodicea felt the need to write a law stating, "If any shall be found to be Judaizers, let them be anathema from Christ," and even today, Christians debate just how much we should follow the Hebrew Scriptures' laws and requirements.

## What Happened in 70 CE?

In the first century CE, the Romans were struggling to retain Judaea as part of the empire. A group of Jews in and around Jerusalem who were not Roman citizens formed into militant political parties that together were known as Zealots. They would actively resist the Roman census and taxation, often claiming their religion as the foundation of the movement. Josephus described them this way: "They have a passion for liberty that is almost unconquerable, since they are convinced that God alone is their leader and master. They think little of submitting to death in unusual forms and permitting vengeance to fall on kinsmen and friends if only they may avoid calling any man master."[3]

Such political turmoil is the backdrop of the Gospels, and it made Jesus's comments, such as "Render to Caesar the things that are Caesar's, and to God the things that are God's" (Mark 12:17), controversial for some listeners.

197

Between April 14 and September 8 in the year 70, Roman general and future emperor Titus besieged Jerusalem. The army quickly destroyed the city's outer walls, but the interior wall remained, trapping the people for months and leading to mass starvation. On August 30, the Roman forces entered and set the second temple on fire. Only Herod the Great's Temple Mount and three towers remained standing.

The destruction of the second temple forced a change in the Jewish religion. As priests were no longer able to offer sacrifices according to the Torah's laws, rabbis focused on Scripture interpretation, synagogue meetings, and ritual practices as the central expressions of worship.

## East Leaves West

The apostles' travels and teachings spread the gospel message of Jesus throughout the Roman Empire, but Christianity got a boost when Constantine I legalized and funded the religion. He called the Council of Nicaea in 325, which brought together Christian leaders from all over his realm. He hoped they would find consensus on deep theological questions such as the nature of Christ and on practical worship activities such as how to observe Passover and Easter. One important unifying document from the council, the Nicene Creed, is recited regularly as Christians' profession of faith.

Five years later, Constantine moved his capital from Rome to "New Rome," which became known as Constantinople and later Istanbul. That city would remain the center of the Byzantine Empire for eleven hundred years, until it was conquered by the Ottoman Empire in 1453.

As Christianity spread throughout the Byzantine Empire, so did theological and political disagreements. Points of contention included issues such as whether clerics should be celibate, if leavened bread was appropriate for communion, and exactly how the Nicene Creed should be worded. But when the bishop of Rome (known as the pope) declared his authority over the patriarch of Constantinople, there was no way to heal the divisions. Rome excommunicated Constantinople, and Constantinople excommunicated Rome in the Great Schism of 1054.

The Eastern and Western churches have never reunited, but in 1965, Pope Paul VI and Patriarch Athenagoras I lifted the excommunications. After a thousand years of separation and distinct growth, the two primary branches of Christianity look very different. Roman Catholicism remains one denomination, but Eastern Orthodoxy is an umbrella over many national churches, each with its own unique traditions, practices, calendars, and deuterocanonical books.

## Protestant Reformations

A quiet perk of going to Harvard is proximity to one of Christianity's great treasures. One night at ten o'clock, after my best friend and I had spent hours inside Widener Library studying for our final exams, the staff inexplicably changed the exit protocols. We were used to handing them books, walking through the magnetic sensors, and picking up our loans at the door. But that night we had to wait in line to exit at closing time. They made us strip off our sixty-pound backpacks, hoist them over the high counter, and wait for them to be searched. "We have to make sure you aren't stealing the Gutenberg Bible!" the librarian deadpanned.

In 1448, Johann Gutenberg built his printing press in Mainz, Germany. His background as a goldsmith helped him in the creation of Europe's first durable type molds, which resembled the backward-facing letters you see on the arms of typewriters. This enabled him to set the text for an entire page of a Bible one time and then print multiple copies from it in ink on paper and vellum.[4]

Gutenberg chose to print Jerome's Latin translation of the Scriptures. This version, known as the Vulgate (which simply means "common tongue"), was commissioned by Pope Damasus I at the end of the fourth century. Its Old Testament was originally based on the Greek Septuagint translation of the Hebrew Bible, but Jerome soon made edits incorporating the Hebrew Masoretic Text. It was edited by later scholars over the next nine hundred years, and Gutenberg's text matches the thirteenth-century version from the University of Paris.

Within twenty years, other printers were producing German translations of the Bible, but the most influential translation—still in use in an updated form today—was published by Martin Luther in 1534. He was a Catholic monk and theology professor who, legend says, nailed a copy of the "Disputation of Martin Luther on the Power and Efficacy of Indulgences" (now commonly called the Ninety-five Theses) onto the door of All Saints Church in Wittenberg, Germany, on October 31, 1517.

What probably started out as a private communication with Luther's local bishop over his concern that the Catholic Church was too money hungry became the pamphlet that launched Protestantism. Instead of reforming the Catholic Church from within, as he seemingly intended to do, a soon-excommunicated Martin Luther would launch a global Christian movement popularizing doctrines that contradicted sixteenth-century Catholicism and somewhat unify Protestant churches to this day. He advocated five principles of biblical interpretation and right theology, commonly called the five *solas*: by Scripture alone, by faith alone, by grace alone, by Christ alone, and by the glory of God alone.

Fourteen years after Luther's excommunication and the same year he published his German translation of the Bible, Henry VIII of England "excommunicated" the Catholic Church from his country. The practices of the Church of England weren't dramatically different from those of the Catholic Church until Henry's son, Edward VI, ushered in the English Reformation. Henry's daughter, Elizabeth I, institutionalized the reforms by signing the Act of Uniformity in 1558, which she intended to bridge the differences between English Catholics and English Protestants.

As the British Empire spread into other nations, so did the Anglican Church. It would go on to be influenced by the thoughts of John Calvin but would retain many Catholic doctrines and practices—such as the formal ordination of bishops, priests, and deacons—which most other Protestant traditions rejected. In America, the Anglican movement developed into the Episcopal Church, while immigrants from other European nations brought with them more Reformed denominations that had also been inspired by John Calvin.

Today, many Protestants will claim one of two Renaissance-era men as their thought leader: John Calvin or Jacob Arminius. Both had their theological claims structured as five points (possibly following the pattern of the five *solas*), and their beliefs seem unable to coexist.

Born in France in 1509, John Calvin was well educated in the fields of philosophy, theology, and law. After converting from Catholicism to Lutheranism and publishing his famous *Institutes of the Christian Religion*, he was run out of France for his Protestant beliefs in 1536. Calvin would live out most of his life in Geneva, where he worked with the city elders to form a theocratic society based on his views of and writings about Scripture. He died in 1564, but his beliefs in the total depravity of humanity, unconditional election, limited atonement, irresistible grace, and the perseverance of the saints were the foundation of Puritanism and influenced theologians such as George Whitefield and Karl Barth.[5]

Jacob Arminius was a toddler in Holland when John Calvin died. He spent his early twenties questioning Calvinism at the Geneva Academy, which Calvin had founded, and he left without achieving a degree. Back home in Holland, while he was working as a minister, Arminius settled his mind that humans must accept God's gift of salvation, Jesus died for everyone, everyone was impacted by Adam and Eve's first sin, grace can be rejected, and salvation can be lost. He died in 1609, but his writings persisted and influenced theologians such as John and Charles Wesley.[6]

When we study the words of our Bibles, we have a tendency to read between the lines. That's how we end up with so many Christians believing Goliath was a giant, Jonah slept inside a whale, and Jesus was born in a barn. Then people with shared beliefs—be they right or wrong—find each other and form groups. And that's how we've ended up with tens of thousands of Christian denominations,[7] each believing they are the only people who understand God correctly. Everyone mistakes consensus for correctness.

All of the arguing and divisiveness comes from following other people's beliefs and not Jesus Himself. Obviously this is not a new problem; following one leader of the Christian movement over another caused division from the moment Jesus resurrected. That is why Paul kept reminding his readers not to follow him or other disciples or apostles but to follow Jesus only (1 Cor. 1:10–17). Paul must be extremely disappointed in how Christians have ignored his advice for the last two thousand years—and Jesus all the more so.

All congregations, regardless of denomination, run the risk of venerating their local pastor or a popular Christian thinker or author. Like Calvin and Arminius, many of today's Christian leaders cannot be blamed for the devotion of their congregations and readers. Some actively preach against the borderline hero worship that made them famous. Others selfishly exploit their positions as leaders by telling congregants what they want to hear in order to grow their numbers and raise donations.

No matter whom you are following—Calvin or Arminius, a worldwide celebrity or your local pastor—the doctrines you adopt from their teachings are not Scripture. So before hanging your faith on the teachings of any human, ask yourself if you would draw the same conclusions about election or prosperity or anything else he or she espouses by simply reading Scripture. Save your faith for what God actually says in the Bible, not what any human says about it.

## Conclusion

One hymn we always seemed to sing at Grandma's church was "My Hope Is Built on Nothing Less." It was written by Edward Mote in 1834 and includes the refrain, "On Christ, the solid Rock, I stand: all other ground is sinking sand." In a book that has focused on physical artifacts—many of which only stood the test of time because they were carved from stone—I want to end with the metaphorical Rock.

A stranger-yet-friend who follows my social media pages once asked me why I do what I do. Why do I spend my days mining history for artifacts that contextualize the Bible? Who really cares how David knocked down Goliath, when and why Persia conquered Babylonia, and what the Temple Mount really is? I care (and I hope you do too!) because physical evidence of the ancient world helps us to understand Scripture better.

We first learn about God from the stories we are told by our churches. Those stories are based on Scripture, yes, but sometimes those stories are far from historical and textual truth. A complete understanding of the Bible—which none of us are likely to achieve in our lifetimes—should be the goal for all Christians. Even though we know Jesus, we should always be seeking a deeper relationship with the historical and spiritual Savior of humanity. Scripture reading strengthens our faith foundations so we can stand confidently and humbly on Jesus's words and work instead of on the shifting sands of opinion, division, popularity, and ideology.

So I encourage you to commit to learning the historical contexts of both Scripture and our Christian faith. Understand why your community believes as it does, but question if your commitment to the veracity of certain doctrines is a result of God's inspiration or human ideas. Strengthen your faith by asking questions and spending time learning the answers. And finally, accept that while on this earth, you will not know everything. But you can trust that our miracle-producing, human-loving God of yesterday, today, and tomorrow does.

# Acknowledgments

An author's work is solitary. Books such as this one require count-less hours of research, writing, and rewriting inside quiet offices with closed doors and giant coffee mugs. But no book is the cre-ation of only one person. I have been taught, inspired, corrected, supported, and loved by so many people throughout my life and career. Without these friends, this book would not exist.

I am thankful to be publishing with the talented team at Revell and Baker Publishing Group. **Rachel McRae** and **Amy Nemecek** are fabulous editors whose insights made this book so much better. Their unique perspectives pushed me to consider ideas differently and express concepts more clearly, and they were always construc-tive and kind when I needed correction. **Chris Kuhatschek** and his team of designers created the perfect cover! It is beautiful, but it also captures the book's content with an artistic expression I could never have imagined. The marketing team led by **Brianna DeWitt** has created opportunities to introduce this book and a better understanding of biblical archaeology to readers all over the world.

**Kathleen Kerr** is not only my agent but also my dear friend. Since 2017 she has advocated for my work, first as an editor and now as my agent. She and Alive Literary Agency helped me find the right publisher for this book, and the Alive team is committed to my professional and personal growth. Without Kathleen's constant encouragement, I would not be writing my own books. That is not an overstatement!

Books are only one way (although the biggest and best way!) that authors speak to their audiences today. I am so grateful for **Danya Clairmont, Stacy Kennedy,** and **Harper Coverston** at Red Bird Social, who taught me how to use social media to find readers who also love archaeology and Scripture. **Tanya Yaremkiv,** my friend and video editor, kept me connected to my audience and perfected content for *The Red-Haired Archaeologist* podcast as I was writing this book.

I was blessed to have passionate and insightful professors during my undergraduate and graduate studies. **Dr. Steven McKenzie, Dr. Baruch Schwartz,** and the late **Dr. Lawrence Stager** not only taught me about Scripture development and biblical archaeology, but they also encouraged me to pursue this work outside of the classroom and share my own love of the ancient Near East with others.

My fellow student and chosen sister, **Melinda Phillips,** was my best buddy at both Rhodes and Harvard. When I can't quite remember a detail from history, she's the first person I call. She listens to my thoughts, gives me her unfiltered opinions, and cares for me as a sister would. When my husband was RIFed as I was finishing this manuscript, she helped us to move to another city— her city—where we are now neighbors.

My very first teachers—my parents **Ross and Dana Womack**— modeled Christian faith and charity every day of my life. They encouraged me (and likely worried over me!) as I chose a field that sometimes takes me to conflict zones on the other side of the world. Today my parents are my most dedicated readers and theology debaters. I praise God that they are also my friends. I am also thankful for my late grandparents, specifically **Donald and Jean Cowan** whom I mentioned in this book. My cousins **Matt** and Tara Cowan (now of "Jonah and the Whale" fame!) also grew up witnessing our grandparents' love for family and faith in God. Thank you, Matt and Tara, for allowing me to share one of your childhood experiences with the world!

I am most humbled by my husband, **David Haley**, who put aside his own graduate school plans to marry me and move to Cambridge, Massachusetts. In the early years, he helped me learn biblical Hebrew by holding my flashcards, he pushed me to travel for my work, and he financially supported me throughout graduate school and continues to provide for our small family today. When he was interviewing for the new job that would eventually move us to Nashville, I overheard him tell a recruiter, "I need a position that allows me to support my wife's career." He has always prioritized our relationship, and that makes him the best partner in life and work I could have.

# Notes

### Introduction: Rocks Are Neither Deaf nor Dumb

1. William Frederic Bade, "Excavation of Tell en-Nasbeh," *Bulletin of the American Schools of Oriental Research* 26, no. 2 (April 1927): 1–7, https://doi.org/10.2307/1354936.

2. "Stonehenge Timeline," The British Museum, accessed March 5, 2024, https://www.britishmuseum.org/exhibitions/world-stonehenge/stonehenge-time line.

3. First Peoples' Assembly of Victoria, "Fact Sheet: Aboriginal Stone Arrangements," First Peoples Relations, Government of Victoria, January 25, 2024, https://www.firstpeoplesrelations.vic.gov.au/fact-sheet-aboriginal-stone-arrangements.

4. Norman Hallendy, "Inuksuk (Inukshuk)," The Canadian Encyclopedia, last edited December 8, 2020, https://www.thecanadianencyclopedia.ca/en/article /inuksuk-inukshuk.

### Chapter 1  Adam and Eve's Creation(s)

1. Titian (Tiziano Vecellio), *Adam and Eve*, c. 1550, oil on canvas, 240 × 186 cm, Museo del Prado, Madrid, https://www.museodelprado.es/en/the-collection /art-work/adam-and-eve/e0ca4331-fb89-47a7-9ba0-be0ece23426b.

2. Sophie Ambler, "Stephen Langton," Magna Carta Trust, accessed January 20, 2025, http://magnacarta800th.com/schools/biographies/magna-carta-bishops /stephen-langton/.

3. Bruce Metzger, *Manuscripts of the Greek Bible: An Introduction to Palaeography* (Oxford University Press, 1981), 41.

4. "About Webb," NASA, accessed March 12, 2024, https://webb.nasa.gov /content/about/index.html.

5. Jonathan O'Callaghan, "How the James Webb Space Telescope Broke the Universe," *MIT Technology Review*, January 21, 2023, https://www.technology review.com/2023/01/21/1065178/james-webb-space-telescope-universe/.

6. Adam Mann, "The James Webb Space Telescope Prompts a Rethink of How Galaxies Form," *Proceedings of the National Academy of Sciences* 120, no. 32 (2023), https://www.pnas.org/doi/10.1073/pnas.2311963120.

7. Richard Elliott Friedman, *Who Wrote the Bible?* (HarperCollins, 1997), 236–37.

8. Joel Achenbach, "Why Carl Sagan Is Truly Irreplaceable," *Smithsonian*, March 2014, https://www.smithsonianmag.com/science-nature/why-carl-sagan-truly-irreplaceable-180949818/#xGIOeQXlqbtmsPPi.99.

9. Carl Sagan, *Cosmos: A Personal Journey*, episode 1, "The Shores of the Cosmic Ocean," aired September 28, 1980, on PBS.

## Chapter 2  Noah's Extraordinary Cruise

1. "Big Butter / Burnt Butter," track 14 on *Heywood Banks Live! Never Trust a Puppet*, recorded at Ann Arbor Comedy Showcase, November 26–28, 2011, https://www.heywoodbanks.com/videos/v/big-butter-jesus.

2. "About the Ark," Ark Encounter, accessed March 18, 2024, https://ark encounter.com/about/.

3. "About," Answers in Genesis, accessed March 18, 2024, https://answers ingenesis.org/about/.

4. "Bible History," Answers in Genesis, accessed March 9, 2025, https://answersingenesis.org/bible-history/.

5. "Nebuchadnezzar Chronicle," *Babylonian Chronicles*, 550BC–400BC, clay tablet, New Babylonian, chronicle for years 605–594 BC, 8.25 × 6.19 cm, British Museum, London, https://www.britishmuseum.org/collection/object/W_1896 -0409-51.

6. "Age of the Earth," Answers in Genesis, accessed March 18, 2024, https://answersingenesis.org/age-of-the-earth/.

7. "Grand Canyon National Park: Geology," National Park Service, last modified February 23, 2024, https://www.nps.gov/grca/learn/nature/grca-geology.htm.

8. National Geographic Society, "How Did Scientists Calculate the Age of Earth?," last modified October 19, 2023, https://education.nationalgeographic .org/resource/how-did-scientists-calculate-age-earth/.

9. "How Does Carbon Dating Work," Beta Analytic Testing Laboratory, accessed March 23, 2024, https://www.radiocarbon.com/about-carbon-dating.htm.

10. Ronald S. Hendel, "The Search for Noah's Flood," *Bible History Daily*, March 27, 2014, https://www.biblicalarchaeology.org/daily/biblical-topics/hebrew -bible/the-search-for-noahs-flood/.

11. Michael D. Coogan, "In the Beginning: The Earliest History," in *The Oxford History of the Biblical World* (Oxford University Press, 2001), 19–23.

12. *The Epic of Gilgamesh*, trans. Maureen Gallery Kovacs (Stanford University Press, 1989), 101–2.

13. "Fact Check: Images of Alleged Giant Human Skeletons Are Altered," Reuters, March 3, 2021, https://www.reuters.com/article/idUSKCN2AV20P/.

14. "Museums of the Mother See," Armenian Apostolic Holy Church Mother See of Holy Etchmiadzin, https://www.armenianchurch.org/en/Museums-at-the -Mother-See.

15. "Noah's Ark? Boatlike Form Is Seen Near Ararat," *Life*, September 5, 1960, 112, 114.

16. "The Discoveries and Archaeological Sites of Ron Wyatt and Wyatt Archaeological Research," Wyatt Archaeological Research, accessed April 4, 2024, https://wyattmuseum.com/.

## Chapter 3 Father Abraham's Many Sons

1. "Vader Abraham met zijn Zeven Zonen," by Pierre Kartner, track 2 on *Vader Abraham en Zijn Goede Zonen*, Elf Provinciën ELF 85.46-G, 1973, 33 rpm.

2. "Biography: Pierre Kartner alias Vader Abraham," Vader Abraham Products, accessed April 9, 2024, https://www.vader-abraham.com/bio_n.html#ontstaan.

3. Jubilees 8:25–30.

4. Cyrus H. Gordon, "Abraham of Ur," in *Hebrew and Semitic Studies Presented to Godfrey Rolles Driver in Celebration of His Seventieth Birthday*, ed. David Winton Thomas and W. D. McHardy (Clarendon, 1963), 77–84.

5. Sir Leonard Woolley, *Excavations at Ur: A Record of Twelve Year's Work* (1900; repr., Kegan Paul, 2006), 128.

6. Megan Sauter, "When Was Jesus Born—B.C. or A.D.? How the Divide Between B.C. and A.D. Was Calculated," *Bible History Daily*, December 9, 2023, https://www.biblicalarchaeology.org/daily/people-cultures-in-the-bible/jesus-historical-jesus/when-was-jesus-born-bc-or-ad/.

7. "Ancient Jericho/Tell es-Sultan," UNESCO World Heritage Convention, accessed April 17, 2024, https://whc.unesco.org/en/list/1687/.

8. To learn more about well-preserved mudbricks, read Danny Rosenberg et al., "7,200 Years Old Constructions and Mudbrick Technology: The Evidence from Tel Tsaf, Jordan Valley, Israel," *PLOS One* 15, no. 1 (January 22, 2020): https://doi.org/10.1371/journal.pone.0227288.

9. "History," The Megiddo Expedition, accessed April 13, 2024, https://www.themegiddoexpedition.com/join-us.

10. D. E. Aune, *Revelation 6–16*, Word Biblical Commentary vol. 52B (Word, 1998), 898–99.

11. *Tel Dan Nature Reserve*, brochure (Israel Nature and Parks Authority Publishing, 2018).

12. Amanda Hope Haley, "Esau's Lost 'Death Right,'" *The Red-Haired Archaeologist* (blog), https://redhairedarchaeologist.com/esaus-lost-death-right/.

## Chapter 4 Joseph's Fall and Rise

1. Really Useful Group, "Joseph and the Amazing Technicolor Dreamcoat: Timeline," Andrew Lloyd Webber Musicals, accessed March 10, 2025, https://www.andrewlloydwebber.com/show/joseph?tab=timeline /.

2. Camilla Turner, "Sir Tim Rice Criticises Teachers for Changing 'Israel' Lyrics in Joseph Musical," *Telegraph*, July 3, 2017, https://www.telegraph.co.uk/news/2017/07/02/sir-tim-rice-criticises-teachers-changing-israel-lyrics-joseph/; Vanessa Thorpe, "Lloyd Webber Backs Tim Rice in Row over 'Political' Change to Musical," *Guardian*, July 8, 2017, https://www.theguardian.com/culture/2017/jul/09/andrew-lloyd-webber-tim-rice-musical-interview-censoring-dreamcoat-lyric.

3. Rosalie David, *Handbook to Life in Ancient Egypt* (Oxford University Press, 1998), 7–10.

4. Chris Stantis et al., "Who Were the Hyksos? Challenging Traditional Narratives Using Strontium Isotope (87Sr/86Sr) Analysis of Human Remains from Ancient Egypt," *PLOS One* 15, no. 7 (July 15, 2020), https://doi.org/10.1371/journal.pone.0235414.

5. Manfred Bietak, *Avaris: The Capital of the Hyksos: Recent Excavations at Tell el-Dabʿa* (British Museum, 1996).

6. Alain Zivie, "Pharaoh's Man, 'Abdiel: The Vizier with a Semitic Name," *Biblical Archaeology Review* 44, no. 4 (2018): 22–31, 64–66.

## Chapter 5 Moses's Big Exit

1. "The Ten Commandments (1956)," AFI Catalog of Feature Films, accessed May 2, 2024, https://catalog.afi.com/Film/52028-THE-TEN-COMMANDMENTS?cxt=filmography.

2. Bava Batra 14b–15a.

3. "'Priestly Benediction' on amulets," 6th century BCE, silver, 3.9–9.7 × 1.1–2.7 cm, Israel Museum, Jerusalem, https://www.imj.org.il/en/collections/198069-0.

4. Hershel Shanks, "Jeremiah's Scribe and Confidant Speaks from a Hoard of Clay Bullae," *Biblical Archaeology Review* 13, no. 1 (1987): 58–65.

5. Julius Wellhausen, *Prolegomena to the History of Israel*, trans. John Sutherland Black and Allan Menzies (Adam and Charles Black, 1885).

6. Christopher Rollston, "Inscriptional Evidence for the Writing of the Earliest Texts of the Bible: Intellectual Infrastructure in Tenth- and Ninth-Century Israel, Judah, and the Southern Levant," in *The Formation of the Pentateuch: Bridging the Academic Cultures of Europe, Israel, and North America*, ed. Jan C. Gertz et al. (Mohr Siebeck, 2016), 15–45.

7. See, for example, Baruch J. Schwartz, "What Really Happened at Mount Sinai?," *Bible Review* 13, no. 5 (1997): 20–30, 46.

8. "The calf and its shrine," 16th century BCE, pottery and silver-plated bronze statuette, 10.5 × 11 cm, model shrine 25 × 12 cm, Israel Museum, Jerusalem, https://www.imj.org.il/en/collections/198013-0.

9. *The Exodus Decoded*, directed by Simcha Jacobovici, aired April 16, 2006, on The History Channel.

10. Hershel Shanks, "The Exodus and the Crossing of the Red Sea, According to Hans Goedicke," *Biblical Archaeology Review* 7 no. 5 (1981): 42–50; John Noble Wilford, "New Find Is Linked to Events to Exodus," *New York Times*, December 24, 1985, https://www.nytimes.com/1985/12/24/science/new-find-is-linked-to-events-to-exodus.html.

11. Bernard F. Batto, "Red Sea or Reed Sea?," *Biblical Archaeology Review* 10, no. 4 (1984): 56–63.

## Chapter 6 David's Duel with a "Giant"

1. *VeggieTales: Dave and the Giant Pickle*, directed by Phil Vischer (Big Idea, 2002), VHS.

2. Katharina Buchholz, "This Is How Much the Global Literacy Rate Grew over 200 Years," World Economic Forum, September 12, 2022, https://www.weforum.org/agenda/2022/09/reading-writing-global-literacy-rate-changed/.

3. "2022 Global Scripture Access," Wycliffe Global Alliance, accessed June 15, 2023, https://www.wycliffe.net/resources/statistics/.

4. Adam S. van der Woude, "Tracing the Evolution of the Hebrew Bible," *Bible Review* 11, no. 1 (1995): 42–45, https://www.baslibrary.org/bible-review/11/1/11.

5. "Plate 1097, Frag 2," *The Leon Levy Dead Sea Scrolls Digital Library*, accessed June 15, 2023, https://www.deadseascrolls.org.il/explore-the-archive/image/B-484181.

6. Aren M. Maier, quoted in Amanda Borschel-Dan, "Colossal Ancient Structures Found at Gath May Explain Origin of Story of Goliath," *Times of Israel*, July 26, 2019, https://www.timesofisrael.com/colossal-ancient-structures-found-at-gath-may-explain-origin-of-story-of-goliath/.

7. Matthew J. Adams and Margaret E. Cohen, "The 'Sea Peoples' in Primary Sources," in *The Philistines and Other "Sea Peoples" in Text and Archaeology*, ed. Ann E. Killebrew and Gunnar Lehmann (Society of Biblical Literature, 2013), 657–59.

8. Trude Dothan and David Ben-Shlomo, "Mycenaean IIIC:1 Pottery in Philistia: Four Decades of Research," in *The Philistines and Other "Sea Peoples" in Text and Archaeology*, 29–36.

9. Michal Feldman et al., "Ancient DNA Sheds Light on the Genetic Origins of Early Iron Age Philistines," *Science Advances* 5, no. 7 (July 3, 2019): 1, https://advances.sciencemag.org/content/5/7/eaax0061.

10. "Foot Combat Armour," 1520, carbon steel, Leeds Castle, Kent, England, https://royalarmouries.org/collection/object/object-19.

11. "Wall panel; relief," 700–692 BC, gypsum, 200.66 × 15 × 238.76 cm, British Museum, London, https://www.britishmuseum.org/collection/object/W_1856-0909-14_1.

## Chapter 7  King Solomon's Disappearance

1. H. Rider Haggard, *King Solomon's Mines* (Cassell, 1855), 22.

2. Haggard, *King Solomon's Mines*, 275–80.

3. Michael D. Danti et al., "Special Report: Current Status of the Tell Ain Dara Temple," *Bible History Daily*, March 9, 2018, https://www.biblicalarchaeology.org/daily/news/special-report-current-status-tell-ain-dara-temple/.

4. "Temple XVI," Tayinat Archaeological Project, https://tayinat.artsci.utoronto.ca/the-toronto-expedition/temple-xvi/; "The Temple," Tel Moza Expedition Project, https://www.telmoza.org/.

5. Philip J. King and Lawrence E. Stager, *Life in Biblical Israel*, Library of Ancient Israel (Westminster John Knox, 2001), 234–36.

6. Inbal Samet, *Megiddo National Park* (brochure), trans. Miriam Feinberg Vamosh (Israel Nature and Parks Authority, n.d.); D. E. Aune, *Revelation 6–16*, Word Biblical Commentary vol. 52B (Dallas: Word, 1998), 898–99.

7. "Battle of Megiddo," National Army Museum, accessed May 21, 2024, https://www.nam.ac.uk/explore/battle-megiddo.

8. Israel Finkelstein and Neil Asher Silberman, *The Bible Unearthed: Archaeology's New Vision of Ancient Israel and the Origin of Its Sacred Texts* (Free Press, 2002); Israel Finkelstein and Eli Piasetzky, "¹⁴C and the Iron Age Chronology Debate: Rehov, Khirbet En-Nahas, Dan, and Megiddo," *Radiocarbon* 48, no. 3 (2006): 373–86.

9. James L. Crenshaw, "Proverbs, Book of," *Anchor Bible Dictionary* 5:513–20.

10. King and Stager, *Life in Biblical Israel*, 45–47, 315–16.

11. "The Harem" and "The March of the Siamese Children," *Rodgers and Hammerstein's The King and I*, directed by Walter Lang (1956; Beverly Hills, CA: 20th Century Fox, 1999), DVD.

12. "Landmarks of the Ancient Kingdom of Saba, Marib," UNESCO World Heritage Convention, accessed May 23, 2024, https://whc.unesco.org/en/list/1700/.

13. *A Modern Translation of the Kebra Nagast (The Glory of Kings)*, trans. and ed. Miguel F. Brooks (Red Sea Press, 2001), xv.

## Chapter 8  Jonah's Whale of a Tale

1. "Tablet," 3300–3100 BC, clay, 8 × 5 cm, British Museum, London, https://www.britishmuseum.org/collection/object/W_1989-0130-2.

2. "Bisotun," UNESCO World Heritage Convention, accessed February 14, 2024, https://whc.unesco.org/en/list/1222/.

3. "Mesopotamian Chronicles," Livius, updated April 14, 2020, https://www.livius.org/sources/about/mesopotamian-chronicles.

4. Joan and David Oates, *Nimrud: An Assyrian Imperial City Revealed* (British School of Archaeology in Iraq, 2001).

5. Carine Harmand, "Sparking the Imagination: The Rediscovery of Assyria's Great Lost City," British Museum, updated February 1, 2019, https://www.britishmuseum.org/blog/sparking-imagination-rediscovery-assyrias-great-lost-city.

6. Stephanie Dalley, "Ancient Mesopotamian Gardens and the Identification of the Hanging Gardens of Babylon Resolved," *Garden History* 21, no. 1 (Summer 1993): 1–13.

7. Doug Fraser, "'I Was Completely Inside': Lobster Diver Swallowed by Humpback Whale off Provincetown," *Cape Cod Times*, June 11, 2021, https://www.capecodtimes.com/story/news/2021/06/11/humpback-whale-catches-michael-packard-lobster-driver-mouth-proviencetown-cape-cod/7653838002/.

8. "Sarcophagus," 3rd century CE, marble, 60 × 192 × 77 cm, British Museum, London, https://www.britishmuseum.org/collection/object/H_1957-1011-1; "Intaglio," 1st century BCE–3rd century CE, glass, British Museum, London, https://www.britishmuseum.org/collection/object/G_1951-0201-1; Jason A. Staples (personal blog), "Stick Man Jonah More Unprecedented Than Previously Realized," accessed May 25, 2024, https://www.jasonstaples.com/bible/stick-man-jonah-more-unprecedented-than-previously-realized/.

## Chapter 9  Israel's Lost Tribes, Temple, and Testimony

1. "'Unto These Hills' Outdoor Drama," Eastern Band of Cherokee Indians, accessed May 31, 2024, https://visitcherokeenc.com/play/attractions/unto-these-hills-outdoor-drama/.

2. National Park Service, "History and Culture," Trail of Tears National Historic Trail, accessed June 1, 2024, https://www.nps.gov/trte/learn/history culture/index.htm; National Park Service, "Cherokee," Great Smoky Mountains National Park, accessed June 1, 2024, https://www.nps.gov/grsm/learn/history culture/cherokee.htm.

3. "About," Native American Indian Association of Tennessee, accessed May 31, 2024, https://naiatn.org/about/.

4. Libby Copeland, "Why Are Americans Obsessed with Genealogy?," *Psychology Today*, October 13, 2020, https://www.psychologytoday.com/us/blog/the -lost-family/202010/why-are-americans-obsessed-genealogy.

5. Sallyann Sack and Amanda Kluveld, "Tracing Jewish Ancestry and Beyond—Exploring the Transformative Impact and Possibilities of the Documentation of Jewish Records Worldwide (DoJR) Project," *Genealogy* 8, no. 2 (2024): 34, https://doi.org/10.3390/genealogy8020034.

6. *Tel Dan Nature Reserve* (brochure), Israel Nature and Parks Authority Publishing, 2018.

7. Thomas H. Maugh II, "Stone Tablet Offers 1st Physical Evidence of Biblical King David," *Los Angeles Times*, August 14, 1993, https://www.latimes.com /archives/la-xpm-1993-08-14-me-23862-story.html.

8. "Obelisk," 825 BC, limestone (black), $45.08 \times 60.96 \times 197.48$ cm, British Museum, London, https://www.britishmuseum.org/collection/object/W_1848 -1104-1.

9. "Stele of Tiglath-Pilesar III (biblical Pul)," 745–727 BCE, dolomite, 240 cm, Israel Museum, Jerusalem, https://www.imj.org.il/en/collections/198926-0.

10. There is some discrepancy over who did the final conquering; Sargon II, the brother of Shalmaneser V, also takes credit for the conquest in his annals, as he ascended the throne the year Samaria fell: "tablet," 7th century BC, clay, $6.9 \times 2.5 \times 12$ cm, British Museum, London, https://www.britishmuseum.org/col lection/object/W_K-1349.

11. "Relief," 700–692 BC, gypsum, $251.46 \times 15 \times 177.80$ cm, British Museum, London, https://www.britishmuseum.org/collection/object/W_1856-0909-14_7.

12. D. J. Wiseman, *Chronicles of the Chaldaean Kings (626–556 B.C.) in the British Museum* (Trustees of the British Museum, 1956), plate 1.

13. Arie Shaus et al., "Ancient Mitochondrial DNA Analysis of an Iron II Burial Cave on the Slope of Tel Kiriath-Yearim," in *New Studies in the Archaeology of Jerusalem and Its Region: Collected Papers*, ed. Yiftah Shalev et al. (Institute of Archaeology of the Hebrew University of Jerusalem, 2023), 16, 49–67, https:// www.researchgate.net/publication/375004626_Ancient_Mitochondrial_DNA _Analysis_of_an_Iron_II_Burial_Cave_on_the_Slope_of_Tel_Kiriath-Yearim.

14. Marinella Bandini, "Mount Nebo, a Story 90 Years Long," *Custodia Terræ Santæ*, July 21, 2023, https://www.custodia.org/en/news/mount-nebo-story-90 -years-long.

15. "Previous Research," Town of Nebo Archaeological Project: Excavations at Khirbat al-Mukhayyat, accessed May 30, 2024, https://www.townofneboproject .com/history/.

16. Paul Raffaele, "Keepers of the Lost Ark?," *Smithsonian*, December 2007, https://www.smithsonianmag.com/travel/keepers-of-the-lost-ark-179998820/.

17. Graham Phillips, *The Templars and the Ark of the Covenant* (Bear, 2004).

## Chapter 10  The Jews' Not-So-Silent Years

1. "Tablet," 547–331 BCE, clay, 6.3 × 7.5 × 2.3 cm, Penn Museum, Philadelphia, https://www.penn.museum/collections/object/372377.
2. Herodotus, *The History*, trans. George Rawlinson (John Murray, 1858), 1.141–216.
3. "Cylinder," 539 BC, fired clay, 21.90–22.80 × 7.80–8.20 × 10 cm, British Museum, London, https://www.britishmuseum.org/collection/object/W_1880-0617-1941.
4. "Bisotun," UNESCO World Heritage Convention, accessed June 6, 2024, https://whc.unesco.org/en/list/1222/.
5. Aaron Demsky, "Who Returned First—Ezra or Nehemiah?," *Bible Review* 12, no. 2 (April 1996): https://library.biblicalarchaeology.org/article/who-returned-first-ezra-or-nehemiah/.
6. Ovid, *Metamorphoses* 1.10.25.
7. Josephus, *Antiquities* 10.8.8–5.
8. Peter Schäfer, *The History of the Jews in Antiquity*, trans. David Chowcat (Harwood Academic, 1995), 6.
9. Schäfer, *History of the Jews in Antiquity*, 8–24.
10. 1 Maccabees 1:41–50.
11. 2 Maccabees 6:2.
12. 1 Maccabees 4:36–59.
13. Schäfer, *History of the Jews in Antiquity*, 124.

## Chapter 11  Jesus's Miraculous Life and Death

1. Amanda Hope Haley, *Barren Among the Fruitful: Navigating Infertility with Hope, Wisdom, and Patience* (Thomas Nelson, 2014).
2. "The Jesus Seminar," Westar Institute, accessed June 26, 2024, https://www.westarinstitute.org/about/the-jesus-seminar.
3. Amy McPherson, "Greccio: The Italian Village That's Home to the World's First Nativity Scene," BBC, December 19, 2023, https://www.bbc.com/travel/article/20231219-greccio-the-italian-village-thats-home-to-the-worlds-first-nativity-scene.
4. Tertullian, *Adversus Marcionem* 3.13.8.
5. Eric Betz, "The Star of Bethlehem: Can Science Explain What It Really Was?," *Astronomy*, last updated February 1, 2024, https://www.astronomy.com/science/the-star-of-bethlehem-can-science-explain-what-it-was/.
6. "About Magdala: The Story," Magdala Tourist Center, accessed June 30, 2024, https://old.magdala.org/about-magdala-2/.
7. Sara Toth Stub, "A 1,000-Year-Old Promise of Peace," BBC, February 24, 2022, https://www.bbc.com/travel/article/20161121-a-1000-year-old-promise-of-peace.
8. "The Holy Fire Ceremony at the Church of the Holy Sepulchre," The Church of the Holy Sepulchre, August 29, 2023, https://thechurchoftheholysepulchre.com/holy-fire-ceremony-in-jerusalem/.

9. Melanie Lidman, "Round-the-Clock Excavations at Church of Holy Sepulchre Yield Historical Treasures," *Times of Israel*, August 9, 2023, https://www.timesofisrael.com/round-the-clock-excavations-at-church-of-holy-sepulchre-yield-historical-treasures/.

10. James D. Tabor, *The Jesus Dynasty: The Hidden History of Jesus, His Royal Family, and the Birth of Christianity* (Simon & Schuster, 2006), 325–31.

11. James D. Tabor, "The Talpiot 'Jesus' Tomb: What's the Latest?" (video), Biblical Archaeology Society Library, https://www.baslibrary.org/videos/talpiot-jesus-tomb-whats-latest; James D. Tabor, "Special Session on *The Jesus Discovery: The New Archaeological Find That Reveals the Birth of Christianity* (New York: Simon & Schuster, 2012)," lecture, Hyatt Regency, Greenville, SC, March 16, 2013.

## Chapter 12  The Church's Growth and Division

1. Anthony J. Saldarini, "Pharisees," *Anchor Bible Dictionary*, 5:298–303; Gary G. Porton, "Sadducees," *Anchor Bible Dictionary*, 5:892–95.

2. Josephus, *Antiquities* 13.9.1.

3. Josephus, *Antiquities* 18.1.6.

4. "The Gutenberg Bible," Harvard Library, accessed July 2, 2024, https://library.harvard.edu/collections/gutenberg-bible.

5. "John Calvin: Father of the Reformed Faith," *Christianity Today*, accessed July 2, 2024, https://www.christianitytoday.com/history/people/theologians/john-calvin.html.

6. "Jacob Arminius," *Christianity Today*, August 8, 2008, https://www.christianitytoday.com/history/people/theologians/jacob-arminius.html.

7. It is difficult to determine the exact number of denominations because survey groups use different criteria. Some will include Mormon, Jehovah's Witness, and Seventh-Day Adventist groups, while others exclude them. Some count every nondenominational church as its own "denomination," and others group them together. When reading any report, do not rely on the headline but review the methods that went into the study. Even numbers have context! One popular source is David B. Barrett, George Thomas Kurian, and Todd M. Johnson, *World Christian Encyclopedia: A Comparative Survey of Churches and Religions in the Modern World*, vol. 1, *The World by Countries: Religionists, Churches, Ministries* (Oxford University Press, 2001), 14.

**AMANDA HOPE HALEY** is a lover of the Bible—its God, its words, its people, and its history. Through her writing and speaking as the Red-Haired Archaeologist, she brings readers and listeners on her journeys to understand artifacts that can contextualize Scripture. She hopes to see all Bible lovers work together to learn history, interpret Scripture, and apply God's Word to their lives.

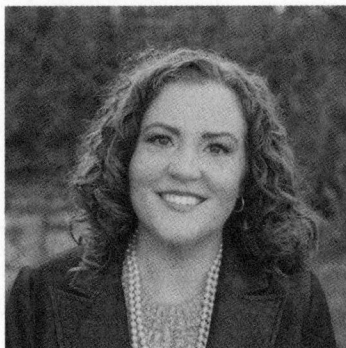

Amanda has a Master of Theological Studies in Hebrew Scripture and Interpretation from Harvard University. She contributed to The Voice Bible as a translator, writer, and editor, and she has been a collaborator for popular Christian authors. Amanda and her husband, David, live in Tennessee with their always-entertaining basset hound, Copper.

=== Connect with Amanda ===

AmandaHopeHaley.com

@AmandaHopeHaley